Weight Watchers New Complete Cookbook #2022

~

Most Effective 1000-Day WW Diet Plan | Delicious Recipes For Your Family

D1416476

Matthew Davis

INTRODUCTION

It's no longer easy now to eat healthy pounds. We are usually persistent, and healthy consumption is inconvenient or expensive. There are a large number of diets that aim to alleviate these problems.

Eat this type of meal, live off grains and dairy, exercise 3 times a week, etc. Diets that promise immediate effects are often not successful. It is very difficult to use, does not close for a long time, and is often dangerous. What should one do?

Weight Watchers is a well-crafted app. Surprisingly, there are no honestly forbidden meals. Statista provides a factor cost per meal that is primarily based entirely on macronutrients such as saturated fat and sugar. It's easier to shed pounds if you stick to that amount. This app has been well checked.

Weight Watchers currently has an app called "Freestyle". Currently, there are new factor-free products or meals that do not interfere with your daily ration. Eggs, poultry, fish, beans and a number of different meals and this allows you to live within your own variety of factors while consuming a lot. There is also the option to carry over your funds every week. You can "save" factors for a unique event if you eat less than weekly factors.

The Freestyle System, a factor-based method, and delicious recipes are outlined in this book. You'll also check reasonable guidelines such as meal prep plans and eat as many factor-free meals as possible. AS you can see in this book our yummy and delicious recipes.

In each one, you may get information on diet and the freestyle factor, due to the fact that healthy consumption and staying within your factors is critical. Millions of people have misplaced weight for Weight Watchers, and maybe you do too!

DESCRIPTION

Are you searching out approaches to observe your weight? Do you need to shed off that more pound and get your lifestyles back? It is time you begin loving yourself and reduce a few slack!

One element which you want to apprehend is that any recipe you've got may be followed right into a weight watchers' recipe.

Yes, this is right! The maximum crucial element is on the way to tweak matters right here and there, lighten it up and hold a near eye in your portions.

Weight looking isn't approximately being uptight, instead, it's far a freestyle application this is aimed toward making sure which you now no longer handiest stay a everyday lifestyles, however additionally consume nicely and love each second of it. Our Book include Delicious Recipes:

• BREAKFAST

• POULTRY

• Mains

• SEAFOOD

• Sides And Snacks

With this and more, you can shed pounds properly and hold them off for as long as you want. These delicious recipes will make it really useful. So, what do you keep preparing for? Come with me and let's lead a whole new lifestyle of fitness and wellness. Have a happy cooking

TABLE OF CONTENT

28. Almond Pancakes

POULTRY

29. Lemon-Garlic & Chicken Zucchini

30. Italian-Balsamic Chicken

31. Enchilada Zucchini Boats

32. Sweet Sour Chicken Rice

33. Oven-Baked Chicken Kebabs

34. WW Chicken Parmesan

35. Creamy Garlic Turkey Soup

36. Chicken Asparagus Sheet Pan

37. Turkey Breasts Stuffed with Pimiento Cheese

38. Turkey Salad

39. Grilled Chicken Breast

40. Buffalo Skillet Turkey

41. Low Carb Chicken Nuggets

42. WW Turkey with Cream Cheese Sauce

43. Chicken Spinach Coconut Curry

44. Turkey Garlic Mushroom Sauté

45. Smokey Mountain Chicken

46. Cauliflower Turkey Casserole

47. Slow-Cooked Chicken Cacciatore

48. Chicken Fajitas

49. Easy Turkey Pot Pie

Mains

50. Avocado Salad

51. Zucchini Dumplings

52. Halloumi Salad

53-Ingredient Tenderloin

54. Honey-Balsamic Pork Roast

55. Peach-Glazed Pork Loin

56. Slow-Cooked Pork Loin & Sweet Onions

57. Pork Chops with Creamy Dijon Sauce

58. Burgers with Mozzarella Inside

59. Mexican Meatza

60. Egg Salad

61. Chicken Soup

62. Broccoli Cream Soup

63. Light & Easy Ham Salad

64. Marmalade-Dijon Ham

65. Slow Cooker Pulled-Pork Tacos

66. Quesadillas

67. Chicken Calzones

68. Taco Pie

69. Soup with Meatballs

70. Cornbread Casserole

71. Roasted Tomato Soup

72. WW Bacon Risotto

73. Easy Lunch Tacos

74. Special Lunch Dish

75. Delightful Bacon Wrapped Sausages

76. Yummy Green Soup

77. Buffalo Wings

78. WW Lunch Burgers

79. Enchilada Bowl

80. Stuffed Tomatoes with Tuna

81. Eggplant Panini

SEAFOOD

82. Ginger-Spiced Halibut

83. Baked Tilapia Spinach

84. Fish Tacos

85. Honey-Lemon Salmon

86. Garlic and Lemon Mahimahi

87. Mediterranean Style Fish

88. Pan-Grilled Fish Steaks

89. Pan-Grilled Tuna Burger

90. Indulgent Seafood Enchiladas

91. Mouth-Watering Seafood Curry

92. Summertime Crab with Napa Cabbage

93. Salmon with Dill and Lemon

94. Grilled Prawn Kebab

95. Cioppino – Seafood Stew

96. Stir-Fried Sesame Shrimp

97. White Fish in Dijon Sauce

98. Fried Salmon Cakes

99. Shrimp Scampi Recipe

100. Shrimp & Tofu Stir Fry

101. Salmon Avocado Salad

102. Shrimp and Avocado Salad

103. Simple Tuna and Cucumber Salad

104. Cheesy and Creamy Tilapia

105. Roasted Mahi-Mahi Fish

106. Prawns in Gravy

107. Buffalo Fish

BREAKFAST

1. Bacon and Lemon spiced Muffins

Preparation Time: 30 mins

Smart Points: three

Servings: 12

Ingredients:

- Lemon thyme, 2 tsps.
- Salt
- Almond flour, three cup.
- Melted butter, ½ cup.
- Baking soda, 1 tsp.
- Black pepper
- Medium eggs, four
- Diced bacon, 1 cup.

Directions:

1. Set a blending bowl in region and stir withinside the eggs and baking soda to comprise nicely.

2. Whisk withinside the seasonings, butter, bacon, and lemon thyme

3. Set the combination in a nicely-coated muffin pan.

4. Set the oven for 20 mins at 3500F, permit to bake

5. Allow the desserts to chill earlier than serving

Nutrition Values: Calories: 186, Fat: 17.1, Fiber: 0.7, Carbs: 1.5, Protein: 7.9

2. Bacon and Seasoned Mushroom Skewers

Preparation Time: 30 mins

Smart Points: three

Servings: 6

Ingredients:

- mushroom caps - 1 pound
- bacon strips - 6
- Salt and ground black pepper, to taste
- candy paprika - ½ teaspoon
- Sweet Mesquite; for seasoning

Directions:

1. Use mushroom caps with salt, pepper, and paprika as seasoning.

2. Spear a bacon strip on a skewer. Spear a mushroom cap, and fold the bacon over it.

3. Continue this technique till you get a mushroom and bacon braid.

4. Do this for the relaxation of the mushrooms and bacon strips.

5. Season with candy mesquite, region all skewers on a grill that has been preheated over medium warmness.

6. Cook for approximately 10 mins, then turn. Cook for every other 10 mins.

7. Divide on special plates and serve.

Nutrition Values: Calories: 47, Fat: 2.5, Fiber: 0.7, Carbs: 2.6, Protein: 3.8

3. Weight Watchers Banana Bread

Prep Time: five mins

Cook: Time:1 hour

Servings: 12

Ingredients

• three mashed bananas

• 1 cup sugar replacement

• 1/3 cup all-cause flour

• half teaspoon salt1

• half teaspoon baking soda

• half cup herbal applesauce

Directions:

1. Preheat the oven to 350 tiers Fahrenheit.

2. Set apart a loaf pan that has been greased.

3. Mash bananas with a fork or a potato masher in a big blending dish.

4. Toss withinside the final elements with an electric powered mixer on medium velocity till completely combined.

5. Pour the combination right into a loaf pan that has been oiled.

6. Preheat oven to 350°F and bake for 50-60 mins. Insert a toothpick or skewer into the middle of the loaf to peer whether or not it is performed. The bread is performed whilst it comes out clean.

7. Allow to chill on a cord rack.

4. Chocolate-Almond Quinoa Breakfast Bars

Serves: 14

Time: About 15 mins

Ingredients:

• 1 cup cooked quinoa

• 12 no-sugar Medjool dates (entire)

• ½ cup coarse almond meal

• ½ cup unsweetened shredded coconut

• 2-three teaspoons water

• ¼ cup semi-candy chocolate chips V

• vegetable oil as needed

Directions:

1. In a meal's processor, pulse the quinoa, dates, almond meal, and coconut till a sticky "batter" form. 2. In a big blending basin, pour the "batter."

2. In a blending bowl, integrate the elements and whisk in teaspoons of water till the combination may be formed into bars.

3. Lay the bars out on an aluminum foil-coated baking pan, spacing them out approximately 12 inches apart. Everything could be OK so long as they do now no longer come into contact with one every other.

4.In a pan, warmness the chocolate chips, stirring constantly, till very well melted. To make the chocolate smooth, a tiny amount of vegetable oil can be required.

5. To finish, drizzle liquid chocolate over the bars.

6. Set the bars withinside the fridge to set.

Nutrition Total calories: 89 Carbs: 10 Protein: 2 Fat: 6 Fiber: 2

5. Butternut Squash & Turkey Sausage

Serves: four

Time: 40-50 mins

Ingredients:

• 1-pound lean ground turkey sausage

• 2 teaspoons more-virgin olive oil

• 2 cups diced butternut squash

• ½ teaspoon garlic powder

• ½ teaspoon Italian seasoning

• ½ teaspoon salt ½ teaspoon black pepper

• four cups clean spinach

• four entire eggs

• four egg whites

Directions:

1. Preheat the oven to four hundred tiers Fahrenheit (2 hundred tiers Celsius).

2. Preheat the cooktop to medium-excessive and region a skillet on pinnacle of it.

3. Once the pan is warm, upload the sausage and cook rotating frequently, till browned.

4. Place the sausage on a serving dish after getting rid of it from the skillet.

5. In a pan, warmness the oil earlier than including the butternut squash.

6. Cook, stirring occasionally, for every other eight to ten mins, or till the squash is smooth.

7. Stir withinside the dry spices and spinach and simmer for 1 minute, or till the spinach has wilted.

8. Combine the eggs and egg whites in a separate bowl.

9. Using cooking spray, grease a baking dish.

10. In a baking dish, layer the sausage, squash, and spinach, then pour the eggs on pinnacle.

11. Bake in a preheated oven for 25-30 mins, or till the eggs are set.

12. Put the meals at the table!

Nutrition Total calories: 331 Carbs: 12 Protein: 33 Fat: 15.5   Fiber: three

6. Veggie Breakfast Casserole

Serves: four

Time: forty mins

Ingredients:

• 6 entire eggs

• ¼ cup mozzarella

• ½ cup chopped onion

• ¼ cup halved cherry tomatoes

• ½ chopped bell pepper

• ½ teaspoon salt

• ½ teaspoon black pepper

• ½ teaspoon Italian seasoning

Directions:

1. Using cooking spray, grease a baking dish.

2. Preheat the oven to 350 tiers Fahrenheit (one hundred eighty tiers Celsius).

3. Whisk collectively the eggs in a big blending bowl, then upload the alternative elements and integrate very well.

4. Transfer the combination to the baking dish you've got prepared.

5. Bake in a preheated oven for 35 mins, or till the eggs are set.

6. Have fun!

Nutrition: calories: 143 Carbs: four Protein: 12 Fat: nine Fiber: 0

7. Easy Egg Muffins

Serves: 6

Time: 30-35 mins

Ingredients:

• 1 teaspoon more-virgin olive oil

• 1 big chopped zucchini

• diced bell pepper

• ½ cup chopped onion eight entire eggs

• Salt to taste

• Black pepper to taste

Directions:

1. In a pan, warmness the oil over medium warmness till it shimmers.

2. Add the zucchini, bell pepper, and onion as soon as they have warmed up.

3. Simmer, stirring occasionally, for approximately 6 mins, or till the greens are tender.

4. Preheat the oven to 350 tiers Fahrenheit (one hundred eighty tiers Celsius).

5. Whisk collectively the eggs in a blending bowl and season with salt and pepper.

6. Using nonstick cooking spray, spray a muffin tray.

7. Evenly distribute the egg desserts most of the muffin cups.

8.Cook at 350 tiers Fahrenheit for 20-25 mins, or till the eggs are set. There could be a few puffiness to them.

9. Put the meals at the table!

Nutrition calories: 121 Carbs: four Protein: nine Fat: 7 Fiber: 0

8. Microwave Cheesy Bacon Egg Grits

Serves: 2

Time: About five mins

Ingredients:

• 2 tablespoons ricotta cheese (fats-unfastened)

• 1 entire egg

• ¼ cup egg whites

• 2 tablespoons dietary yeast

• 2 tablespoons crumbled bacon Salt to taste

• Black pepper to taste

• eight-oz. warm water

• 2 packets Quaker cheese grits

Directions:

1. Using cooking spray, coat a microwave-secure blending bowl.

2 - Combine all elements, besides the boiling water and grits, in a big blending bowl.

3. Microwave at excessive calories for 1 minute.

4. Microwave for 1 minute more, stirring occasionally.

5. Pour the recent water over the grits and punctiliously blend them collectively.

6.After stirring for two mins, make certain the grits are similarly saturated.
6.

7. Finally, provide it a terrific swirl earlier than serving!

Nutrition: calories: 221 Carbs: 24 Protein: 15 Fat: five Fiber: 1

9. Cottage-Cheese Pancakes with Raspberry Jam

Serves: four

Time: About 15 mins

Ingredients:

• eight entire eggs

• 1 cup cottage cheese (decreased fats)

• four tablespoons almond flour

• four tablespoons coconut flour

• ½ teaspoon natural vanilla extract

• ½ teaspoon baking soda Pinch of salt

• four tablespoons unsweetened almond milk

• four tablespoons raspberry jam

Directions:

1. Combine all the elements in a blender (besides the almond milk).

2. Blend till smooth, including almond milk as had to get the favored batter consistency.

3.When a drop of water is dropped at the griddle or pan, it sizzles.

4. For every pancake, pour 14 cup of batter onto the griddle.

5.When the center of the pancake starts to bubble and the rims are performed, flip it.

6. Continue to warmness till the potatoes are golden brown.

7. Before serving, toss every pancake with 1 tablespoon of jam!

Nutrition calories: 326 Carbs: 10 Protein: 23 Fat: 14 Fiber: 6

10. Blueberry-Almond Oats

Serves: four

Time: 20-25 mins

Ingredients:

• 2 cups water

• 1 cup 1% milk

• 1 teaspoon natural almond extract

• 2 tablespoons honey

• ½ cup dry steel-reduce oats

• 1 cup frozen blueberries Pinch of salt

Directions:

1. Bring the water, milk, almond extract, and honey to a boil in a saucepan over excessive warmness.

2. Add the oats and blueberries to the boiling water.

3. Reduce the warmth to low and simmer for every other 10 mins, stirring occasionally.

4. Season with salt and pepper.

5. Cook for every other three-five mins, or till the oats attain the favored texture.

6. Finally, provide it a terrific swirl and serve!

Nutrition calories: 149 Carbs: 31 Protein: five Fat: 2 Fiber: 2.75

11. Lemon Raspberry Oats

Serves: 2

Time: 2 ½ mins

Ingredients:

• 6 tablespoons short oats

• 1 cup unsweetened vanilla almond milk

• ½ cup frozen raspberries

• 1 teaspoon lemon zest Stevia to taste

Directions:

1. Combine all the elements in a microwave-secure blending bowl.

2. Microwave on excessive for two mins.

three. Give it a terrific stir.

four. Put the meals at the table!

Nutrition

calories: 137 Carbs: 25 Protein: three Fat: four Fiber: 2

12. Weight Watchers Egg Muffins

Total Time: 25 mins

Servings: 12

Ingredients

• 12 eggs

• four tbs water

• 1 C. Veggie crumbles (cooked in step with bundle directions) I used morning big name farms (three points)

• 1 C. Finely chopped tomatoes

• 1 C chopped clean spinach

• 1 tsp garlic powder½

• tsp onion powder

• ½ tsp ground black pepper¼

• tsp salt

Directions:

1. Preheat the oven to 350 tiers Fahrenheit.

2. In a medium blending basin, crack the eggs.

3. In a blending bowl, integrate the flour, baking soda, and water.

4. Stir withinside the different elements till they're very well included with the egg combination.

5. Using nonstick spray, coat a 12-slot muffin pan.

6. Fill 12 muffin tins with the egg combination.

7. Bake for 18-22 mins, or till golden brown on the edges and the tops have set.

Nutrition Calories: 96kcal | Carbohydrates: 3g | Protein: 9g | Fat: 5g | Saturated Fat: 1g | Cholesterol: 163mg | Sodium: 198mg | Potassium: 161mg | Fiber: 1g

13. Easy Protein Balls Recipe

Total Time:2 hours

Servings:12

Ingredients

• 1 cup Peanut Butter

• ½ cup Protein Powder

• ⅓ cup Honey

• 2 tsp Vanilla Extract

• ½ cup Peanut optional

For Chocolate Coating

• three-ounce Baking Chocolate unsweetened

• three tbsp Honey or confectioners swerve sweetener

• 1 tbsp Olive Oil

Directions:

1. To begin, whisk collectively all the elements, consisting of peanut butter, protein powder, sweetener, and vanilla extract. In a meals processor or blender, integrate all the elements till they shape a smooth dough.

2. (If you do not like or do not have protein powder, you could use almond flour or coconut flour on your keto diet.)

3. Then, the usage of that smooth dough, create 1-inch balls and positioned them in a unmarried layer on a baking sheet or plate. (If the dough seems to be too smooth, upload extra protein powder or flour to tighten it up.) If time is of the essence, use low-fats or dairy-unfastened milk to melt and tenderize the dough.)

4. To make the combination less assailable and much less sticky, freeze the balls for 20-30 mins.

Coating in chocolate

1. To make chocolate coating, integrate chocolate, sweetener, and coconut oil in a blending bowl. Put all of those elements in a microwave-secure bowl and warmth for 30 seconds at a time till melted and creamy.

2. Remove the peanut butter balls from the freezer and set them apart. Using a toothpick, pierce the peanut butter balls and pour the melted chocolate over them. Remove the toothpick from the lined balls and set them on parchment paper. Freeze those balls for as a minimum 1 hour once more.

3. Remove them from the freezer and function a dessert or snack. So yummy and delectable!

Nutrition Calories: 110kcalCarbohydrates: 2gProtein: 4gFat: 9gSaturated Fat: 2gSodium: 10mgFiber: 2gSugar: 1g

14. Mouth-watering Breakfast Pie

Preparation Time: fifty-five mins

Smart Points: three

Servings: eight

Ingredients:

• 3/4-pound red meat; ground

• half onion; chopped.

• 1 pie crust

• three tablespoons taco seasoning

• 1 teaspoon baking soda

• Mango salsa for serving

• half purple bell pepper; chopped.

• A handful cilantro; chopped.

• eight eggs

• 1 teaspoon coconut oil

• Salt and black pepper to the taste.

Directions:

1. Heat up a pan with the oil over medium warmness; upload red meat, cook till it browns and mixes with salt, pepper and taco seasoning.

2. Stir once more, switch to a bowl and go away apart for now.

3. Heat up the pan once more over medium warmness with cooking juices from the meat, upload onion and bell pepper; stir and cook for four mins

4. Add eggs, baking soda and a few salts and stir nicely.

5. Add cilantro; stir once more and take off warmness.

6. Spread red meat blend in pie crust, upload greens blend and unfold over meat, introduce withinside the oven at 350 tiers F and bake for forty-five mins

7. Leave the pie to calm down a bit, slice, divide among plates and serve with mango salsa on pinnacle.

Nutrition Values: Calories: 198; Fat: 11; Fiber: 1; Carbs: 12; Protein: 12

15. Chicken Omelet

Preparation Time: 20 mins

Smart Points: three

Servings: 1

Ingredients:

- 2 bacon slices; cooked and crumbled

- 2 eggs

- 1 tablespoon self-made mayonnaise

- 1 tomato; chopped.

- 1 ounce rotisserie fowl; shredded

- 1 teaspoon mustard

- 1 small avocado; pitted, peeled and chopped.

- Salt and black pepper to the taste.

Directions:

1. In a bowl, blend eggs with a few salt and pepper and whisk gently.

2. Heat up a pan over medium warmness; spray with a few cooking oil, upload eggs and cook your omelet for five mins

3. Add fowl, avocado, tomato, bacon, mayo and mustard on one 1/2 of the omelet.

4. Fold omelet, cowl pan and cook for five mins more

5. Transfer to a plate and serve

Nutrition Values: Calories: 398; Fat: 32; Fiber: 6; Carbs: 5; Protein: 25

16. Special Almond Cereal

Preparation Time: five mins

Smart Points: 2

Servings: 1

Ingredients:

- 2 tablespoons almonds; chopped.

- 1/4 cup coconut milk

- 1 tablespoon chia seeds

- 2 tablespoon pepitas; roasted

- A handful blueberries

- 1 small banana; chopped.

- 1/4 cup water

Directions:

1. In a bowl, blend chia seeds with coconut milk and go away apart for five mins

2. In your meal's processor, blend 1/2 of the pepitas with almonds and pulse them nicely.

3. Add this to chia seeds blend.

4. Also upload the water and stir.

5. Top with the relaxation of the pepitas, banana portions and blueberries and serve

Nutrition Values: Calories: 199; Fat: 3; Fiber: 2; Carbs: 4; Protein: 5

17. Awesome Avocado Muffins

Preparation Time: 30 mins

Smart Points: 2

Servings: 12

Ingredients:

• 6 bacon slices; chopped.

• 1 yellow onion; chopped.

• half teaspoon baking soda

• half cup coconut flour

• 1 cup coconut milk

• 2 cups avocado; pitted, peeled and chopped.

• four eggs

• Salt and black pepper to the taste.

Directions:

1. Heat up a pan over medium warmness; upload onion and bacon; stir and brown for a few mins

2. In a bowl, mash avocado portions with a fork and whisk nicely with the eggs

3. Add milk, salt, pepper, baking soda and coconut flour and stir everything.

4. Add bacon blend and stir once more.

5. Grease a muffin tray with the coconut oil, divide eggs and avocado blend into the tray, introduce withinside the oven at 350 tiers F and bake for 20 mins

6. Divide desserts among plates and serve them for breakfast.

Nutrition Values: Calories: 199; Fat: 7; Fiber: 5; Carbs: 7; Protein: 6

18. Tasty WW Pancakes

Preparation Time: 15 mins

Smart Points: three

Servings: four

Ingredients:

• 2 oz. cream cheese

- 1 teaspoon stevia

- half teaspoon cinnamon; ground

- 2 eggs

- Cooking spray

Directions:

1. In your blender, blend eggs with cream cheese, stevia and cinnamon and mix nicely.

2. Heat up a pan with a few cooking spray over medium excessive warmness; pour 1/3 of the batter, unfold nicely, cook for two mins, turn and cook for 1 minute more

3. Transfer to a plate and repeat the movement with the relaxation of the batter.

4. Serve them proper away.

Nutrition Values: Calories: 344; Fat: 23; Fiber: 12; Carbs: three; Protein: sixteen

19. WW Salad in A Jar

Preparation Time: 10 mins

Smart Points: 2

Servings: 1

Ingredients:

- 1-ounce preferred veggies

- 1-ounce purple bell pepper; chopped.

- 4 oz. rotisserie fowl; kind of chopped.

- four tablespoons more virgin olive oil

- half scallion; chopped.

- 1 ounce cucumber; chopped.

- 1 ounce cherry tomatoes; halved

- Salt and black pepper to the taste.

Directions:

1. In a bowl, blend veggies with bell pepper, tomatoes, scallion, cucumber, salt, pepper and olive oil and toss to coat nicely.

2. Transfer this to a jar, pinnacle with fowl portions and serve for breakfast.

Nutrition Values: Calories: 179; Fat: 12; Fiber: 5; Carbs: 4.5; Protein: 17

20. WW Breakfast Cereal

Preparation Time: thirteen mins

Smart Points: 1

Servings: 2

Ingredients:

- half cup coconut; shredded

- 1/4 cup macadamia nuts; chopped.

- four teaspoons ghee

- 2 cups almond milk

- 1 tablespoon stevia
- 1/4 cup walnuts; chopped.
- 1/4 cup flax seed
- A pinch of salt

Directions:

1. Heat up a pot with the ghee over medium warmness; upload milk, coconut, salt, macadamia nuts, walnuts, flax seed and stevia and stir nicely.

2. Cook for three mins; stir once more, take off warmness and go away apart for 10 mins

3. Divide into 2 bowls and serve

Nutrition Values: Calories: 140; Fat: three; Fiber: 2; Carbs: 1. 9; Protein: 7

21. Yummy Smoked Salmon

Preparation Time: 20 mins

Smart Points: 2

Servings: three

Ingredients:

- four eggs; whisked
- half teaspoon avocado oil
- four oz. smoked salmon; chopped.
- For the sauce:
- half cup cashews; soaked; drained

- 1/3 cup inexperienced onions; chopped.
- 1 teaspoon garlic powder
- 1 cup coconut milk
- 1 tablespoon lemon juice
- Salt and black pepper to the taste.

Directions:

1. In your blender, blend cashews with coconut milk, garlic powder and lemon juice and mix nicely.

2. Add salt, pepper and inexperienced onions, combo once more nicely, switch to a bowl and maintain withinside the refrigerator for now.

3. Heat up a pan with the oil over medium-low warmness; upload eggs, whisk a bit and cook till they're nearly performed

4. Introduce on your preheated broiler and cook till eggs set.

5. Divide eggs on plates, pinnacle with smoked salmon and serve with the inexperienced onion sauce on pinnacle.

Nutrition Values: Calories: 193 Fat: 10; Fiber: 2; Carbs: 11; Protein: 15

22. Almond Coconut Cereal

Preparation Time: five mins

Smart Points: 2

Servings: 2

Ingredients:

- Water, 1/4 cup.

- Coconut milk, 1/4 cup.

- Roasted sunflower seeds, 2 tbsps.

- Chia seeds, 1 tbsp.

- Blueberries, ½ cup.

- Chopped almonds, 2 tbsps.

Directions:

1. Set a medium bowl in role to feature coconut milk and chia seeds then reserve for 5 mins

2. Plug in and set the blender in role to combo almond with sunflower seeds

3. Stir the mixture to chia seeds combination then upload water to combine evenly.

4. Serve crowned with the final sunflower seeds and blueberries

Nutrition Values: Calories: 181, Fat: 15.2, Fiber: four, Carbs: 10.5, Protein: 4.7

23. Almond Porridge

Preparation Time: 15 mins

Smart Points: 2

Servings: 1

Ingredients:

- Ground cloves, ¼ tsp.

- Nutmeg, ¼ tsp.

- Stevia, 1 tsp.

- Coconut cream, ¾ cup.

- Ground almonds, ½ cup.

- Ground cardamom, ¼ tsp.

- Ground cinnamon, 1 tsp.

Directions:

1. Set your pan over medium warmness to cook the coconut cream for some mins

2. Stir in almonds and stevia to cook for five mins

3. Mix in nutmeg, cardamom, and cinnamon

4. Enjoy whilst nevertheless warm

Nutrition Values: Calories: 695, Fat: 66.7, Fiber: 11.1, Carbs: 22, Protein: 14.three

24. Asparagus Frittata Recipe

Preparation Time: forty mins

Smart Points: 2

Servings: four

Ingredients:

- Bacon slices, chopped: four
- Salt and black pepper
- Eggs (whisked): eight
- Asparagus (trimmed and chopped): 1 bunch

Directions:

1. Heat a pan over medium warmness, upload bacon, stir and cook for five mins.

2. Add asparagus, salt, and pepper, stir and cook for every other five mins.

3. Add the chilled eggs, unfold them withinside the pan, allow them to stand withinside the oven and bake for 20 mins at 350° F.

4. Share and divide among plates and serve for breakfast.

Nutrition Values: calories 251, carbs 14, fats 6, fiber 8, protein 7

25. Avocados Stuffed with Salmon

Preparation Time: 10 mins

Smart Points: 2

Servings: 2

Ingredients:

- Avocado (pitted and halved): 1
- Olive oil: 2 tablespoons

- Lemon juice: 1
- Smoked salmon (flaked): 2 oz.
- Goat cheese (crumbled): 1 ounce
- Salt and black pepper

Directions:

1. Combine the salmon with lemon juice, oil, cheese, salt, and pepper on your meals processor and pulsate nicely.

2. Divide this combination into avocado halves and serve.

3. Dish and Enjoy!

Nutrition Values: calories 300m, fats 15, fiber five, carbs eight, protein sixteen

26. Bacon and Brussels Sprout Breakfast

Preparation Time: 22 mins

Smart Points: three

Servings: three

Ingredients:

- Apple cider vinegar, 1½ tbsps.
- Salt
- Minced shallots, 2
- Minced garlic cloves, 2
- Medium eggs, three

- Sliced Brussels sprouts, 12 oz.

- Black pepper

- Chopped bacon, 2 oz.

- Melted butter, 1 tbsp.

Directions:

1. Over medium warmness, short fry the bacon till crispy then reserve on a plate

2. Set the pan on hearthplace once more to fry garlic and shallots for 30 seconds

3. Stir in apple cider vinegar, Brussels sprouts, and seasoning to cook for 5 mins

4. Add the bacon to cook for 5 mins then stir withinside the butter and set a hollow on the middle

5. Crash the eggs to the pan and permit cook completely

6. Enjoy

Nutrition Values: Calories: 275, Fat: 14.8, Fiber: 5.5, Carbs: 17.2, Protein: 17.5

27. Strawberry Smoothie

Serves: four

Time: five mins

Ingredients:

- ½ cup immediate oatmeal

- 1 ½ cups skim milk

- 1 cup frozen strawberries

- 60 grams unsweetened protein powder

- ¼ teaspoon vanilla extract

Directions:

1. Puree all the elements in a blender till smooth.

2. Blend till the combination is absolutely smooth.

3. Put the meals at the table!

Nutrition: calories: 150 Carbs: 21 Protein: 17.5 Fat: 1.9 Fiber: 2.6

28. Almond Pancakes

Preparation Time: 20 mins

Smart Points: three

Servings: 12

Ingredients:

- 6 eggs

- 1/3 cup almonds; toasted

- 2 oz. cocoa chocolate

- 1 teaspoon almond extract

- 1/4 cup coconut; shredded
- half teaspoon baking powder
- 1/3 cup coconut oil
- half cup coconut flour
- 1/3 cup stevia
- 1 cup almond milk
- Cooking spray
- A pinch of salt

Directions:

1. In a bowl, blend coconut flour with stevia, salt, baking powder and coconut and stir.

2. Add coconut oil, eggs, almond milk and the almond extract and stir nicely once more.

3. Add chocolate and almonds and whisk nicely once more.

4. Heat up a pan with cooking spray over medium warmness; upload 2 tablespoons batter, unfold into a circle, cook till it's golden, turn, cook once more till it's performed and switch to a pan.

5. Repeat with the relaxation of the batter and serve your pancakes proper away.

Nutrition Values: Calories: 266; Fat: 12; Fiber: 7.5; Carbs: 10; Protein: 11

POULTRY

29. Lemon-Garlic & Chicken Zucchini

Serves: four

Time: 15-21 mins

Ingredients:

- 2 tablespoons flour
- 1 teaspoon lemon-pepper seasoning
- 1 teaspoon garlic powder
- ½ teaspoon salt
- 1⅓ kilos boneless skinless chicken tenderloin
- 1 tablespoon extra-virgin olive oil
- three cups chopped zucchini
- ½ cup chicken inventory
- 1 tablespoon apple cider vinegar

Directions:

1. Whisk collectively the flour, lemon-pepper seasoning, garlic powder, and salt in a blending dish.

2. Using your fingers, dredge the tenderloins withinside the aggregate till very well covered.

3. In a medium saucepan, warmth the oil till it shimmers.

4. Add the chicken to the pan as soon as it is warm and cook for two-three mins in keeping with facet, or till golden brown.

5. Place the plate at the desk for the time being.

6. Add the zucchini to the new pan and cook for three mins, stirring regularly.

7. Pour withinside the inventory and vinegar, scraping any meals portions caught to the lowest of the pan to deglaze it.

8. Return the chicken to the skillet and simmer for five-10 mins on low warmth, or till the inner temperature reaches 170 ranges.

9. Put the meals at the desk!

Nutrition: calories: 241 Carbs: 11 Protein: 40 Fat: 6 Fiber: 1

30. Italian-Balsamic Chicken

Serves: four

Time: 17-25 mins

Ingredients:

• 1 ⅓   kilos boneless skinless chicken breasts

• 2 teaspoons Italian seasoning

• 1 teaspoon salt

• 1 teaspoon black pepper

• 2 teaspoons extra-virgin olive oil eight-oz sliced mushrooms

• three minced garlic cloves

• ½ cup chicken inventory

• 2 ½ tablespoons top balsamic vinegar

Directions:

1. Season chicken breasts to flavor with Italian seasoning, salt, and pepper.

2. In a pan, warmth the oil over medium warmth till it shimmers.

3. Add the chicken to the pan as soon as it's far warm and cook for simplest 2 to a few mins in keeping with facet on every facet.

4. Put it on preserve for the time being.

5. Cook for three-four mins, stirring regularly, till mushrooms are softened.
6. Remove the pan from the warmth and set it aside.

6. Deglaze the pan through scraping away any burned-on meals bits which have collected earlier than pouring withinside the chicken inventory and balsamic vinegar.

7. Return the chicken to the skillet and cook for every other 10-15 mins on low warmth, or till it reaches one hundred sixty five ranges at the inside.

8. Put the meals at the desk!

**Nutrition: calories: 215
Carbs: 5 Protein: 34 Fat: 6
Fiber: 1**

31. Enchilada Zucchini Boats

Ingredients:

- Big pot of water

- 2 medium-sized zucchinis

- ½ teaspoon extra-virgin olive oil

- ¼ cup chopped onion

- ½ teaspoon Italian seasoning

- ¼ teaspoon chili powder

- ½ tablespoon tomato paste

- eight-oz cooked + shredded chicken breasts Pinch of salt

- Pinch of black pepper

- ⅓ cup reduced-fats shredded cheddar cheese

Sauce:

- 2 minced garlic cloves

- ½ chopped chipotle Chile in adobo sauce

- ¾ cup tomato sauce

- ¼ teaspoon taco seasoning

- ⅓ cup chicken inventory Pinch of salt

Directions:

1. Sauté the garlic in a small skillet over medium warmth for about thirty seconds, or till fragrant.

2. Bring the final components to a boil whilst usually stirring.

3. Reduce the warmth to low and go away to simmer for 10 mins.

4. While the sauce is cooking, carry a pot of water to a boil.

5. Preheat the oven to four hundred ranges Fahrenheit (two hundred ranges Celsius).

6. Cut the zucchinis lengthwise in 1/2 of and scoop off sufficient flesh to depart a 14-inch shell at the bottoms.

7. Remove the zucchini flesh from the zucchini and chop it into tiny portions.

8. To cook zucchini, blanch it in a pot of boiling water for 1 minute earlier than putting off it from the water.

9. For the time being, set it aside.

10. In a separate pan, warmth the olive oil over medium warmth.

11. Add the onion to the new oil and cook for a couple of minutes, or till it's far not raw.

12. Combine the chopped zucchini flesh and the final components in a blending bowl till the tomato paste is absolutely absorbed.

13. Add the shredded chicken after a couple of minutes of tossing and absolutely blend.

14. Cook for every other three mins, tossing once in a while and seasoning with salt and pepper as required.

15. To make the inspiration in your boats, pour 1 1/four cup of the sauce right into a massive baking dish.

16. Arrange the boats on a degree surface, hollowed facet up, and lightly fill with the chicken aggregate.

17. Drizzle the relaxation of the home-made enchilada sauce on pinnacle and pinnacle with cheese.

18. Wrap aluminum foil across the baking dish.

19. Preheat the oven to 350 ranges Fahrenheit.

20. It's time to serve!

Nutrition: calories: 116 Carbs: 10.5 Protein: 12 Fat: 5.5 Fiber: 6

32. Sweet Sour Chicken Rice

Serves: eight

Time: 50-60 mins

Ingredients:

• 2 kilos boneless skinless chicken breasts

• 1 tablespoon extra-virgin olive oil

• 2 chopped inexperienced onions

• ¼ cup ketchup

• ¼ cup honey

• 2 tablespoons soy sauce

• 1 teaspoon ground ginger

• 1 teaspoon ground garlic

• 1 teaspoon salt

• ⅓ cup apple cider vinegar

• 2 pouches Uncle Ben's entire-grain rice

Directions:

1. Combine the chicken and the final components (besides the rice) in a Ziploc bag and seal it.

2. Squish the chicken on your fingers to make certain the marinade is nicely distributed.

3. After putting off from the oven, relax for at the least half-hour.

4. Pour the contents of the bag right into a baking dish whilst the timer is going off.

5. Bake for 20-25 mins at 425 ranges Fahrenheit, or till the chicken reaches an inner temperature of 160 ranges Fahrenheit.

6. Serve with rice at the facet!

Nutrition: calories: 197
Carbs: 10.7 Protein: 26
Fat:43 Fiber: 5

33. Oven-Baked Chicken Kebabs

Serves: four

Time: forty mins

Ingredients:

- ¼ cup clean parsley

- 2 limes' really well worth of juice

- 2 tablespoons extra-virgin olive oil three minced garlic cloves

- 1 teaspoon salt

- 1 teaspoon taco seasoning

- 1 ⅓ kilos boneless chicken breasts

- 2 yellow chopped bell peppers

- Handful of cherry tomatoes

- 1 chopped onion

Directions:

1. Blend the parsley, lime juice, oil, garlic, salt, and taco seasoning till easy in a blender.

2. Cube the chicken and integrate it with the marinade in a bag. three. Refrigerate for at the least one night.

3. After putting off from the oven, relax for at the least half-hour.

4. To cook withinside the oven, preheat the oven to broil.

5. Immediately skewer the marinated chicken bell pepper portions, cherry tomatoes, and onion chunks onto skewers and serve.

6. Bake for five mins on one facet, then turn and bake for every other five mins, or till kebabs are nicely cooked.

7. Check the temperature of the chicken to decide if it has reached 155 ranges.

8. Put the meals at the desk!

Nutrition: calories: 265
Carbs: 10.5 Protein: 33 Fat: 9
Fiber: 5

34. WW Chicken Parmesan

Smart Points: four

Servings: three

Preparation time: 60 mins

Ingredients

- ¾ cup parmesan cheese

- 1 oz. red meat rinds

- 1 pound chicken breasts

- Salt, black pepper, oregano and garlic powder

• ½ cup marinara sauce

Directions

1. Preheat the oven to 3600F.

2. Put 1/2 of parmesan cheese and the red meat rinds in a meals processor and system till coarse.

3. Transfer this aggregate right into a dish and dredge the chicken breasts.

4. Season the chicken breasts with salt, black pepper, oregano and garlic powder.

5. Transfer into the oven and bake for approximately 25 mins till golden brown in color.

6. Remove from the oven and pour marinara sauce over every chicken breast.

7. Top with the final parmesan cheese and go back to the oven.

8. Bake for approximately 15 extra mins and dish out to serve warm.

Nutrition Values:

Calories 357

Total Fat 14.3g

Saturated Fat five.7g

Cholesterol 131mg

Sodium 691mg

Total Carbohydrate 7.7g

Dietary Fiber 1.4g

Total Sugars 4.9g

Protein 48.1g

35. Creamy Garlic Turkey Soup

Smart Points: three

Servings: four

Preparation time: 30 mins

Ingredients

• 2 cups turkey, shredded

• 2 tablespoons butter, melted

• 1 cup heavy cream

• Garlic seasoning and salt, to flavor

• 14.5 ounces chicken broth

Directions

1. Heat butter over medium warmth in a saucepan and upload shredded turkey.

2. Coat with melted butter and upload heavy cream, chicken broth and garlic seasoning.

3. Mix nicely and convey to a boil.

4. Reduce warmth to low and simmer for approximately four mins.

5. Season with salt and serve warm.

Nutrition Values:

Calories 290

Total Fat 21g

Saturated Fat eleven.9g

Cholesterol 109mg

Sodium 428mg

Total Carbohydrate 2.1g

Dietary Fiber 0g

Total Sugars 0.3g

Protein 23.3g

36. Chicken Asparagus Sheet Pan

Smart Points: three

Servings: eight

Preparation time: forty mins

Ingredients

• ½ pound asparagus, trimmed

• 2 kilos chicken breasts, reduce in 1/2 of to make four skinny portions

• four sundried tomatoes, reduce into strips

• eight provolone cheese slices

• Salt and black pepper, to flavor

Directions

1. Preheat the oven to 4000F and grease a massive sheet pan.

2. Arrange chicken breasts and asparagus at the sheet pan and pinnacle with sundried tomatoes.

3. Season with salt and black pepper and switch to the oven.

4. Bake for approximately 25 mins and put off from the oven.

5. Top with provolone cheese slices and bake for approximately three extra mins.

6. Dish out and serve warm.

Nutrition Values:

Calories 322

Total Fat 15.9g

Saturated Fat 7.1g

Cholesterol 120mg

Sodium 364mg

Total Carbohydrate 2.3g

Dietary Fiber 0.7g

Total Sugars 1.1g

Protein 39.7g

37. Turkey Breasts Stuffed with Pimiento Cheese

Smart Points: three

Servings: four

Preparation time: forty mins

Ingredients

• 1 tablespoon pimientos, sliced and chopped

• Paprika, salt and black pepper, divided

• ½ cup Gouda cheese, smoked and shredded

• four small boneless, skinless turkey breasts, trimmed

• 1 tablespoon extra-virgin olive oil

Directions

1. Preheat the oven to 4000F.

2. Mix collectively pimientos, Gouda cheese and paprika in a bowl.

3. Cut slits withinside the turkey breasts horizontally and upload the pimientos aggregate in the slits.

4. Season the turkey breasts with paprika, salt and black pepper.

5. Heat oil over medium excessive warmth in a massive ovenproof skillet and upload turkey.

6. Cook for approximately 2 mins on every facet till browned and switch to the oven.

7. Bake for approximately 15 mins and put off from the oven to serve warm.

Nutrition Values:

Calories 270

Total Fat 10.9g

Saturated Fat 6.5g

Cholesterol 102mg

Sodium 288mg

Total Carbohydrate 2.9g

Dietary Fiber 0.4g

Total Sugars 2.1g

Protein 35.4g

38.Turkey Salad

Serves: 6

Time: 35 mins

Ingredients:

• 2 cups shredded and cooked turkey breast meat

• ½ cup nonfat undeniable Greek yogurt

• ¼ cup nonfat bitter cream

• 1 tablespoon low-fats mayonnaise

• three chopped celery stalks

• 1 tablespoon dill pickle relish

• 1 teaspoon garlic powder

• 1 teaspoon onion powder

• ½ teaspoon paprika

• ½ teaspoon salt

Directions:

1. In a massive blending basin, integrate all the components.

2. Refrigerate the aggregate for 1/2 of an hour to gain the nice effects.

3. Put the meals at the desk.

Nutrition: calories: 192 Carbs: 5 Protein: 17 Fat: 10 Fiber: 0

39. Grilled Chicken Breast

Smart Points: 1

Servings: four

Preparation time: forty five mins

Ingredients

• three tablespoon extra-virgin olive oil

• ¼ cup balsamic vinegar

• 2 teaspoons dried rosemary and thyme

• Kosher salt and black pepper, to flavor

• four chicken breasts

Directions

1. Preheat grill to medium excessive warmth.

2. Whisk collectively balsamic vinegar, olive oil, dried rosemary, dried thyme, kosher salt and black pepper in a bowl.

3. Reserve approximately one fourth of the marinade and upload chicken breasts withinside the marinade.

4. Mix nicely and permit it to marinate for approximately half-hour.

5. Transfer chicken to the grill and cook for approximately 6 mins on every facet, basting with reserved marinade.

6. Remove from the grill and serve on a platter.

Nutrition Values:

Calories 373

Total Fat 21.4g

Saturated Fat four.5g

Cholesterol 130mg

Sodium 127mg

Total Carbohydrate 0.5g

Dietary Fiber 0.3g

Total Sugars 0.1g

Protein 54.3g

40. Buffalo Skillet Turkey

Smart Points: 2

Servings: four

Preparation time: 25 mins

Ingredients

• four boneless skinless turkey breasts

- three tablespoons butter

- eight slices muenster cheese

- Garlic powder, cayenne pepper, kosher salt and black pepper

- 1 cup buffalo sauce

Directions

1. Heat 1/2 of the butter over medium warmth in a massive skillet and upload turkey.

2. Season with garlic powder, kosher salt and black pepper.

3. Cook for approximately five mins on every facet till golden and dish out on a plate.

4. Heat the relaxation of the butter withinside the equal skillet and upload cayenne pepper and buffalo sauce.

5. Return the turkey to the skillet and pinnacle with 2 slices of muenster cheese on every breast.

6. Cover with a lid and cook for approximately three mins till the cheese is melted.

7. Dish out and serve warm.

Nutrition Values:

Calories 389

Total Fat 26g

Saturated Fat sixteen.2g

Cholesterol 77mg

Sodium 653mg

Total Carbohydrate 1.5g

Dietary Fiber 0.3g

Total Sugars 0.8g

Protein 37.3g

41. Low Carb Chicken Nuggets

Smart Points: 2

Servings: 6

Preparation time: 25 mins

Ingredients

- ¼ cup mayonnaise

- 2 medium chicken breasts

- 1 cup blanched almond flour

- 2 tablespoons olive oil

- Sea salt and black pepper, to flavor

Directions

1. Put the chicken withinside the salted water for approximately 10 mins.

2. Drain it and reduce the chicken into nugget sized portions.

3. Put mayonnaise in a single bowl and blend almond flour, sea salt and black pepper in every other bowl.

4. Coat every chicken nugget with mayonnaise and dredge withinside the almond flour aggregate.

5. Heat oil over medium excessive warmth in a skillet and upload chicken nuggets in a unmarried layer.

6. Cook for approximately three mins in keeping with facet till golden and dish out to serve.

Nutrition Values:

Calories 283

Total Fat 20.4g

Saturated Fat 2.8g

Cholesterol 46mg

Sodium 118mg

Total Carbohydrate 6.3g

Dietary Fiber 2g

Total Sugars 0.6g

Protein 18.2g

42. WW Turkey with Cream Cheese Sauce

Smart Points: three

Servings: eight

Preparation time: 35 mins

Ingredients

• 20 oz. turkey breast

• Salt and black pepper, to flavor

• 2 tablespoons butter

• three cups cream cheese

• 1 tablespoon tamari soy sauce

Directions

1. Season the turkey generously with salt and black pepper.

2. Heat butter in a massive pan over medium warmth and upload turkey breasts.

3. Cook for approximately 6 mins on every facet and stir in cream cheese and tamari soy sauce.

4. Cook for approximately 15 mins on medium low warmth and dish out to serve warm.

Nutrition Values:

Calories 404

Total Fat 34.4g

Saturated Fat 21.2g   1

Cholesterol 134mg

Sodium 1123mg

Total Carbohydrate five.4g

Dietary Fiber 0.4g

Total Sugars 2.7g

Protein 18.9g

43. Chicken Spinach Coconut Curry

Smart Points: 2

Servings: 6

Preparation time: five hours 10 mins

Ingredients

• 2 tablespoons curry paste

• 1 onion, finely sliced

• 1 pound chicken cubed

• 800 g clean spinach, chopped

• four hundred ml coconut cream

Directions

1. Put all of the components in a sluggish cooker and stir nicely.

2. Lock the lid and cook on High Pressure for approximately five hours.

3. Dish out in a serving bowl and serve warm.

Nutrition Values:

Calories 341

Total Fat 21.9g

Saturated Fat 15g

Cholesterol 58mg

Sodium 164mg

Total Carbohydrate eleven.7g

Dietary Fiber four.8g

Total Sugars three.6g

Protein 27.7g

44. Turkey Garlic Mushroom Sauté

Smart Points: 2

Servings: four

Preparation time: 30 mins

Ingredients

• 1 cup mushrooms, sliced

• three tablespoons butter, divided in 1/2 of

• 1½ kilos turkey thighs, skinless and boneless

• Sea salt and black pepper, to flavor

• three garlic cloves, minced

Directions

1. Season the turkey with sea salt and black pepper.

2. Heat 1/2 of butter over medium excessive warmth in a massive skillet and upload turkey.

3. Cook for approximately 6 mins on every facet and dish out on a plate.

4. Heat the relaxation of the butter withinside the skillet and upload garlic and mushrooms.

5. Sauté for approximately five mins and stir withinside the cooked turkey.

6. Sauté for approximately three mins and dish out to serve.

Nutrition Values:

Calories 357

Total Fat 23.9g

Saturated Fat five.5g

Cholesterol 84mg

Sodium 184mg

Total Carbohydrate 1.3g

Dietary Fiber 0.2g

Total Sugars 0.3g

Protein 32.7g

45. Smokey Mountain Chicken

Smart Points: three

Servings: eight

Preparation time: 30 mins

Ingredients

• 1 cup low carb Barbecue sauce

• 1½ cups provolone cheese, sliced

• 2 kilos chicken breast, boneless and skinless

• ½ pound bacon, cooked

• ½ cup mozzarella cheese, shredded

Directions

1. Preheat the grill to medium excessive warmth.

2. Grill chicken for approximately eight mins over medium warmth.

3. Drizzle with barbeque sauce and turn the bird.

4. Baste the alternative facet with the barbeque sauce and layer with bacon strips, mozzarella and provolone cheese slices.

5. Cover the grill and cook for approximately 2 extra mins till the cheese is melted.

6. Remove from the grill and serve warm.

Nutrition Values:

Calories 421

Total Fat 21.7g

Saturated Fat eight.3g

Cholesterol 122mg

Sodium 1290mg

Total Carbohydrate 12.3g

Dietary Fiber 0.2g

Total Sugars 7.3g

Protein 41.4g

46. Cauliflower Turkey Casserole

Smart Points: three

Servings: four

Preparation time: 35 mins

Ingredients

- 1 tablespoon Italian seasoning
- 2 cups cauliflower rice, uncooked
- 2 cups cooked turkey, diced
- ¼ cup heavy whipping cream
- ½ cup parmesan and garlic cheese

Directions

1. Preheat the oven to 3600F and grease a casserole dish with nonstick cooking spray.

2. Mix collectively cauliflower rice, Italian seasoning and turkey in a massive bowl.

3. Transfer this aggregate into the organized casserole dish.

4. Combine cream, parmesan and garlic cheese in every other bowl till combined.

5. Pour over the cauliflower rice aggregate and switch to the oven.

6. Bake for approximately 20 mins and put off from the oven to serve warm.

Nutrition Values:

Calories 184

Total Fat 7.3g

Saturated Fat 4.4g

Cholesterol 66mg

Sodium 114mg

Total Carbohydrate 6.1g

Dietary Fiber 0g

Total Sugars 2.3g

Protein 22.6g

47. Slow-Cooked Chicken Cacciatore

Serves: four

Time: 6 hours, 10 mins

Ingredients:

- 2 kilos boneless skinless chicken breast
- 1 teaspoon salt
- 1 teaspoon black pepper five minced garlic cloves
- ½ chopped onion
- 28-oz overwhelmed tomatoes 1 chopped yellow bell pepper
- four- oz sliced shiitake mushrooms 1 tablespoon Italian seasoning

Directions:

1. Season the chicken breasts nicely with salt and pepper.

2. Before including the components, preheat a skillet and coat it with cooking spray.

3. On each aspect of the pan, sear the chicken for two mins on every facet.

4. In a sluggish cooker, integrate all the components.

5. Add the garlic and onion to the new pan and cook for approximately four mins, stirring regularly.

6. Combine the components in a sluggish cooker with the final components and simmer for six hours on low.

7. Before changing the duvet at the saucepan, supply it a lively stir.

8. Cook for six hours at the low putting at a low temperature.

9. Check to peer if the chicken has reached one hundred sixty five ranges whilst the timer is going off.

10. Put the meals at the desk!

Nutrition: calories: 220 Carbs: 10 Protein: 31 Fat: 6 Fiber: 2

48. Chicken Fajitas

Serves: four

Time: forty-forty-five mins

Ingredients:

• 1 tablespoon cumin

• 2 teaspoons garlic powder

• 1 teaspoon onion powder

• 1 teaspoon salt

• 1 teaspoon paprika

• ½ teaspoon chili powder

• 1-pound boneless skinless chicken breasts

• 1 cubed tomato

• 1 sliced yellow bell pepper

• 1 sliced candy onion

• four reduced-calorie tortillas

Directions:

1. Preheat the oven to 375 ranges Fahrenheit (one hundred ninety ranges Celsius).

2. Using cooking spray, grease a baking dish.

3. Combine the dry spices in a massive blending dish.

4. To finish, thinly slice the chicken breasts and coat them withinside the spice aggregate.

5.In a baking dish, region the pro chicken and cowl it with the tomatoes, bell peppers, and onion.

6. Bake for 35-forty mins, or till the chicken reaches 155 ranges at the inside.

7. Serve the chicken and greens straight away wrapped in low-calorie tortillas.

**Nutrition: calories: 188
Carbs: 14.5 Protein: 31 Fat:4
Fiber: 1**

49. Easy Turkey Pot Pie

Ingredients:

• 2 cups frozen combined greens

• 2 cups chopped and cooked turkey breast meat

• Two (10 ¾-ounce) cans of reduced-fats cream of mushroom soup

• 1 cup reduced-fats baking blend (Bisques')

• ½ cup 1% milk

• 1 entire egg

• 1 teaspoon onion powder 1 teaspoon black pepper

• ½ teaspoon garlic powder

Directions:

1. Preheat oven to four hundred ranges Fahrenheit and oil an eight-through-eight-inch baking dish.

2. Combine the greens, turkey, and mushroom soup in a massive blending dish.

3.Making the topping is as clean as combining the baking blend with the milk, egg, and spices in a separate bowl.

4 Drizzle the dressing over the turkey and greens.

5.Bake the pan for half-hour or till the topping is golden brown.

6. Make positive it is warm whilst you serve it!

**Nutrition: calories: 255
Carbs: 37 Protein: 12 Fat: 7
Fiber: 5.8**

Mains

50. Avocado Salad

Preparation time: 10 mins

Cooking time: five mins

Smart Points: 1

Servings: 2

Ingredients:

• 1 cup arugula lettuce

• three ounces. bacon, sliced

• ½ avocado, chopped

• 1 tablespoon lemon juice

• 1 teaspoon olive oil

• 1 tablespoon almonds, chopped

• 1 teaspoon coconut milk

Directions:

1. Chop the sliced avocado kind of and toss it withinside the skillet. Roast it for five mins.

2. When the bacon begins off evolved to be crunchy, its miles cooked.

3. Add the bacon withinside the salad bowl.

4. Add chopped avocado and almonds.

5. Make the seasoning: blend up collectively coconut milk, olive oil, and lemon juice.

6. Pour the seasoning over the salad and blend it up.

Nutrition Values: Calories 402, fats 32.7, fiber 5.5, carbs 7.5, protein 20

51. Zucchini Dumplings

Preparation time: 15 mins

Cooking time: 15 mins

Smart Points: 2

Servings: 6

Ingredients:

• three zucchinis

• 1 cup ground red meat

• 1 teaspoon ground black pepper

• ½ teaspoon chili flakes

• 1 teaspoon olive oil

• ½ teaspoon garlic powder

Directions:

1. Trim zucchini and reduce them to get skinny slices.

2. Mix up collectively ground red meat, ground black pepper, chili flakes, and garlic powder.

3. Make the crosses from the sliced zucchini and placed the small quantity of ground red meat combination withinside the center of each cross.

4. Twrapthem to get the form of dumplings and switch at the baking dish. Sprinkle the dumplings with olive oil.

5. Cook them withinside the preheated to 375F oven for 15 mins.

Nutrition Values: Calories 179, fats 11.5, fiber 1.2 carbs 4.7, protein 14.7

52. Halloumi Salad

Preparation time: 10 mins

Cooking time: five mins

Smart Points: 1

Servings: four

Ingredients:

• 10 Oz Halloumi cheese

• 1 teaspoon olive oil

- ½ teaspoon chili flakes

- 1 tablespoon lime juice

- 1 cup lettuce, kind of chopped

- 1 cucumber, chopped

- 1 tablespoon avocado oil

- 1 teaspoon sesame seeds

Directions:

1. Sprinkle cheese with olive oil and chili flakes.

2. Grill cheese for two mins from every length. Then chop the cheese kind of and switch withinside the salad bowl.

3. Add chopped lettuce, cucumber, and sesame seeds.

4. Sprinkle the salad with lime juice and avocado oil. Mix it up.

Nutrition Values: Calories 193, fats 14.1, fiber 0.7, carbs 6.5, protein 12.2

53-Ingredient Tenderloin

Serves: four

Time: 25-33 mins

Ingredients:

- 1 ¼ kilos red meat tenderloin

- 1/four cup Shiro (white) miso paste

- ⅛ cup liquid monk fruit extract

Directions:

1. Preheat the pinnacle rack of your broiler to the very best putting available.

2. In a blending dish, integrate the miso paste and liquid stevia. It's possible that you may want to cook the miso paste for some seconds withinside the microwave to melt it up sufficient to combo.

3. Spread a miso-stevia paste all around the tenderloin's surface.

4. Broil for 10 mins, turning midway through, in a roasting pan lined with aluminum foil.

5.If the red meat would not acquire a temperature of as a minimum 150 levels after some other eight mins of broiling, rotate after four mins.

6. When the red meat reaches one hundred forty five levels, get rid of it from the oven and set apart for 10 mins to relaxation.

7. Cut into slices and serve with a zero-factor vegetable like inexperienced beans.

Nutrition: Calories: 186 Carbs: 5.6Protein: 30 Fat: 5 Fiber: 0

54.Honey-Balsamic Pork Roast

Serves: eight

Time: four-6 hours, five mins

Ingredients:

- 2 kilos boneless red meat pinnacle loin roast
- 1 teaspoon salt
- 1 teaspoon black pepper
- ½ teaspoon garlic powder
- ⅓ cup low-sodium vegetable broth
- ⅓ cup suitable balsamic vinegar
- ¼ cup apple cider vinegar
- 1 tablespoon honey

Directions:

1. Before setting the red meat roast withinside the sluggish cooker, season it with salt, pepper, and garlic.

2. Stir withinside the vegetable inventory nicely.

3. Whisk collectively the vinegars and honey in a blending dish till very well combined.

4. Drizzle the sauce on pinnacle of the roast.

5. Cover and cook on low for four-6 hours, or till the red meat reaches one hundred forty five levels.

6. Serve with the aid of using reducing into portions.

Nutrition: Calories: 207 Carbs: 5 Protein: 23 Fat: 10 Fiber: 0

55.Peach-Glazed Pork Loin

Serves: five

Time: 60 mins

Ingredients:

- 2 cups Smucker's sugar-unfastened peach preserves
- 1 ½ kilos boneless red meat loin
- ½ teaspoon salt
- ½ teaspoon black pepper
- ½ teaspoon paprika

Directions:

1. Preheat the oven to 500 levels Fahrenheit (one hundred eighty levels Celsius).

2. Position the pinnacle oven rack as near the oven's pinnacle as feasible without permitting the roast to return back into contact with the heating element.

3.Heat the preserves in a microwave-secure bowl for 10-20 seconds, or till they may be barely thinned out. There's a risk you may want a few waters.

4. Preheat the oven and line a roasting pan with layers of aluminum foil.

5. Use a nonstick frying spray to coat the pan.

6. Before serving, season the roast with salt, pepper, and paprika.

7. Apply the jam on the beef with a pastry brush.

8. Bake for 50 mins, checking after 15 mins to make certain the preserves do not end up too darkish on pinnacle. Browning is in incredible condition.

9. Remove the red meat from the oven whilst it reaches 150 levels and permit it relaxation for five mins.

10. Serve with the aid of using reducing the cake into portions.

Nutrition: Calories: 244 Carbs: 32 Protein: 17 Fat: three Fiber: 0

56. Slow-Cooked Pork Loin & Sweet Onions

Serves: four

Time: 10-12 hours

Ingredients:

• 2 ½ kilos sliced candy onions

• 2 tablespoons melted mild butter

• 2 teaspoons brown sugar

• three minced garlic cloves

• 2 tablespoons flour

• 1 ¾ kilos boneless red meat loin

• 2 packets onion soup + dip blend (Lipton Recipe Secrets)

Directions:

1. Combine the onions, butter, sugar, and garlic in a sluggish cooker and cook on low for eight hours.

2. Preheat the oven to four hundred levels Fahrenheit and bake for 12 hours.

3. Add the flour and retain to cook stirring periodically, for some other half-hour.

4. Place the red meat loin on pinnacle of the onions and cowl with the soup and dip combination.

5. Cook for eight to ten hours on low warmness.

6. When the timer is going off, end shredding the beef with forks.

7. Garnish with a sprinkling of onions at the aspect!

Nutrition: Calories: 414 Carbs: 31 Protein: 27 Fat: 7 Fiber: 0

57. Pork Chops with Creamy Dijon Sauce

Serves: four

Time: 13-15 mins

Ingredients:

• Four (four-ounce) center-reduce red meat loin chops

• ½ teaspoon salt

• ½ teaspoon black pepper

• ½ teaspoon onion powder

• ⅓ cup fats-unfastened fowl inventory

• 1 ½ tablespoons Dijon mustard

• ⅓ cup nonfat 1/2 of-and-1/2 of

• Pinch of dried thyme

Directions:

1. Before cooking the red meat, season it with salt, pepper, and onion powder.

2. Coat a huge pan in nonstick cooking spray and warmth on medium-excessive.

3. When the pan is warm, upload the chops and cook for three-four mins consistent with aspect, or till accomplished.

4. Remove the fowl to a plate in the intervening time as soon as it's been properly browned. Pork ought to be cooked to a temperature of 150 levels Fahrenheit.

5. Pour the liquid into the skillet to deglaze it, scraping away any closing chunks of meat.

6. Combine the mustard and 1/2 of-and-1/2 of in a big blending bowl.

7. To thicken the sauce, lessen the warmth to low and simmer for some other 7 mins.

8. Add a twig of thyme to end.

9. Before serving, pour the sauce over the beef!

Nutrition: Calories: 274 Carbs: 2 Protein: 28 Fat: sixteen Fiber: 0

58. Burgers with Mozzarella Inside

Preparation time: 15 mins

Cooking time: 15 mins

Smart Points: 2

Servings: four

Ingredients:

• 2 cups ground red meat

• 1 teaspoon dried dill

• 1 teaspoon dried oregano

• ½ teaspoon ground black pepper

• ½ cup Mozzarella balls

• 1 tablespoon butter

• 1 tablespoon coconut flour

• ½ teaspoon salt

• ½ teaspoon chili flakes

- ¼ cup of water

Directions:

1. Put ground red meat, dried oregano, ground black pepper, coconut flour, salt, and chili flakes withinside the blending bowl.

2. Mix up the combination.

3. Make eight balls from the beef combination. Put Mozzarella ball internal each meatball. Press them lightly to get burger form.

4. Transfer the burgers at the baking dish. Add butter and water.

5. Cook the meal withinside the preheated to the 360F oven for 15 mins. The cooked burgers ought to have a golden-brown color.

Nutrition Values: Calories 225, fats 15.5, fiber 1, carbs 1.5, protein 18.8

59. Mexican Meatza

Preparation time: 10 mins

Cooking time: 18 mins

Smart Points: 2

Servings: 2

Ingredients:

- ¼ cup ground red meat
- 1/three cup ground red meat
- five ounces. chorizo
- 1 tablespoon Enchilada sauce
- 1 teaspoon taco seasoning
- ½ tomato, diced
- ¼ cup lettuce leaves, chopped

Directions:

1. Line the baking tray with the baking paper. Preheat the oven to 365F.

2. Mix up collectively ground red meat, ground red meat chorizo, Enchilada sauce, and taco seasoning.

3. Place the beef combination withinside the baking tray and flatten it to get the beef layer.

4. Transfer the tray withinside the oven and cook it for 15 mins.

5. Then upload diced onions and lettuce leaves. Cook the meal for three mins greater.

6. Remove Meatza from the oven and sit back until the room temperature.

7. Cut it into the servings.

Nutrition Values: Calories 498, fats 38.1, fiber 1.1, carbs five.2, protein 31.5

60. Egg Salad

Preparation time: 10 mins

Cooking time: eight mins

Smart Points: three

Servings: four

Ingredients:

- four eggs
- 2 tablespoon mayonnaise
- ¼ cup clean dill, chopped
- 1 avocado, chopped
- 1 teaspoon lime juice
- ¼ teaspoon ground black pepper
- 1 cup water, for cooking

Directions:

1. Pour water withinside the saucepan, upload eggs and near the lid.

2. Boil the eggs for eight mins.

3. Meanwhile, withinside the salad bowl integrates collectively avocado and chopped dill.

4. When the eggs are cooked, sit back them withinside the ice water and peel.

5. Chop the eggs and upload withinside the salad combination.

6. Sprinkle the salad with lime juice, ground black pepper, and mayonnaise.

7. Mix up the salad carefully.

Nutrition Values: Calories 202, fats 15.5, fiber 4.5, carbs 7.5, protein 7.2

61. Chicken Soup

Preparation time: 10 mins

Cooking time: 25 mins

Smart Points: three

Servings: five

Ingredients:

- three cups of water
- five fowl drumsticks
- 1 bell pepper, chopped
- ½ white onion, diced
- 1 eggplant, chopped
- 1 teaspoon olive oil
- ½ teaspoon salt
- ½ teaspoon chili pepper
- ¾ cup heavy cream
- 1 tablespoon dried oregano

Directions:

1. Pour water withinside the saucepan. Add drumsticks and near the lid.

2. Boil it for 10 mins.

3. Then upload chopped bell pepper, onion, salt, chili pepper, and dried oregano. Cook it for five mins over the medium warmness.

4. Meanwhile, pour olive oil withinside the skillet and preheat it. Add chopped eggplants and roast them on excessive

warmness for three mins. Stir them from time to time.

5. Add the roasted eggplants withinside the soup.

6. Add heavy cream. Cook the soup for 10 mins greater over the medium-low warmness.

7. When the soup is cooked, permit it relaxation for 10-15 mins earlier than serving.

Nutrition Values: Calories 186, fats 10.8, fiber 5.2, carbs 5.9, protein 14.5

62. Broccoli Cream Soup

Preparation time: 10 mins

Cooking time: 15 mins

Smart Points: 2

Servings: 2

Ingredients:

• ½ cup heavy cream

• ½ cup of water

• 1 cup broccoli florets

• ¼ white onion, diced

• ¼ teaspoon garlic, diced

• three ounces. Cheddar cheese, shredded

• 1 ounces. bacon, fried, chopped

• 1 teaspoon butter

• 1 teaspoon dried cilantro

• ¾ teaspoon cayenne pepper

Directions:

1. Pour water and heavy cream withinside the saucepan. Bring the liquid to boil.

2. Add broccoli florets, diced onion, garlic, butter, dried cilantro, and cayenne pepper.

3. Boil the combination for 10 mins or till the broccoli is cooked.

4. Then upload shredded cheese and boil it for three mins greater.

5. When the cheese is melted, combo the soup with the assist of the hand blender till you get a creamy texture.

6. Ladle soup withinside the bowls and sprinkle with fried bacon.

Nutrition Values: Calories 392, fats 33.5, fiber 1.7, carbs 6.5, protein 18

63. Light & Easy Ham Salad

Serves: four

Time: 35 mins

Ingredients:

- 1 tablespoon mango chutney

- 2 tablespoons mild mayo

- 2 tablespoons simple nonfat Greek yogurt

- 2 teaspoons dried mustard

- 2 teaspoons onion powder

- 1 cup chopped + cooked ham

Directions:

1. Pulse all the components (besides the ham) in a meals processor till smooth, approximately 30 seconds.

2. Add the ham to the creamy sauce and pulse till absolutely combined in case you need smaller ham bits for your salad.

3. Refrigerate for half-hour in a nicely sealed container.

4. Serve atop cucumber slices to save you including more points.

Nutrition: Calories: 75 Carbs: 4.6 Protein: 7.5 Fat: 5.5 Fiber: 0

64.Marmalade-Dijon Ham

Serves: sixteen

Time: 2 hours, five mins

Ingredients:

- tablespoons orange marmalade

- 2 tablespoons Dijon mustard

- One (6-7 pound) absolutely-cooked, smoked spiral reduce ham

Directions:

1. Preheat the oven to 325 levels Fahrenheit (one hundred eighty levels Celsius).

2. To put together the glaze, whisk collectively four tablespoons orange marmalade and all the mustard.

3. Brush the glaze all around the ham in a huge roasting pan coated with aluminum foil.

4. Cook for two hours, or 20 mins consistent with pound of red meat, till accomplished withinside the oven.

5. half-hour earlier than the give up of the cooking period, baste with the leftover orange marmalade.

6. Serve with the aid of using reducing the cake into portions.

Nutrition: Calories: 155 Carbs: 12 Protein: 15 Fat: 7 Fiber: 0

65. Slow Cooker Pulled-Pork Tacos

Serves: four

Time: eight-nine hours, five mins

Ingredients:

- 1-pound red meat tenderloin

- 15-oz tomato sauce

- 1 tablespoon cumin

- 1 tablespoon chili powder

- 1 tablespoon brown sugar

- ½ teaspoon paprika

- ½ teaspoon salt

- three minced garlic cloves

- eight (6-inch) corn tortillas

- ½ cup reduced-fats shredded Mexican cheese

- 1 diced tomato

- Shredded lettuce to taste

Directions:

1.Put the beef withinside the sluggish cooker first.

2. In a blending dish, integrate the tomato sauce and the closing components, as much as and such as the garlic.

3. Pour sufficient liquid into the sluggish cooker to very well cowl the beef.

4. Cook, stirring regularly, on low for eight-nine hours.

5. Combine the red meat shreds with the sauce. 6.

6. heat the tortillas and bring together the tacos with 34 cup red meat, 14 cup tomato, and a pair of tablespoons cheese in every taco. You may also eat as plenty lettuce as you choose.

Nutrition: Calories: 232 Carbs: 15 Protein: 29 Fat: 6 Fiber: 3

66. Quesadillas

Preparation time: 10 mins

Cooking time: eight mins

Smart Points: 2

Servings: four

Ingredients:

- 7 ounces. fowl breast, cooked shredded

- ½ avocado, sliced

- 1 white onion, sliced

- 1 bell pepper, sliced

- 1 tablespoon olive oil

- ½ teaspoon ground black pepper

- four ounces. Monterey Jack cheese, shredded

- five ounces. Cheddar cheese, shredded

Directions:

1. Preheat skillet nicely.

2. Pour olive oil withinside the skillet and upload sliced onion and bell pepper.

3. Cook the veggies for five mins over the medium warmness. Stir them from time to time.

4. Then line the baking tray with parchment.

5. Mix up collectively Monterey Jack cheese and Cheddar cheese.

6. Make the wholes from cheese at the parchment (tortilla size and bake for three-four mins or till golden brown.

7. Chill the cheese little.

8. Place sliced avocado, shredded fowl, and cooked veggies at the cheese tortillas and roll them withinside the form of quesadillas.

9. Roast it for 30 seconds from every aspect after which reduce into servings.

Nutrition Values: Calories 408, fats 30.1, fiber 2.7, carbs 7.5, protein 27.5 s

67. Chicken Calzones

Preparation time: 15 mins

Cooking time: forty mins

Smart Points: three

Servings: four

Ingredients:

• eight ounces. fowl breast, boneless, skinless

• ½ teaspoon olive oil

• ½ teaspoon ground black pepper

• ½ teaspoon salt

• 6 ounces. Parmesan cheese, grated

• 1 cup almond flour

• four tablespoon butter

• 2 eggs, whisked

• 1 tablespoon clean parsley, chopped

• 2 tablespoon marinara sauce

Directions:

1. Make the calzone dough: withinside the blending bowl, integrate collectively almond flour and butter. Knead the gentle dough.

2. Cut the dough into 2 parts.

3. Then rub the fowl breast with olive oil, ground black pepper, and salt.

4. Place it withinside the oven and bake for 25 mins at 360F.

5. Remove the cooked fowl breast from the oven and chop it.

6. Combine the fowl with marinara sauce, chopped parsley, and whisked eggs.

7. Line the parchment withinside the baking tray. Place one a part of the

dough withinside the tray and roll it up with the assist of the rolling pin.

8. Then vicinity the fowl combination at the dough.

9. Roll up the closing dough and vicinity it over the fowl. Secure the rims of the dough. Pin the dough with the assist of the knife or fork and switch withinside the preheated to the 360F oven.

10. Cook calzone for 15 mins. The cooked calzone ought to have a mild brown color.

11. Cut it into the servings.

Nutrition Values: Calories 387, fats 28.6, fiber 1.1, carbs 6.5, protein 30.5

68. Taco Pie

Preparation time: 10 mins

Cooking time: 25 mins

Smart Points: three

Servings: 6

Ingredients:

• 2 cups ground red meat

• 1 tablespoon Taco seasoning

• 1 tablespoon butter

• 1/3 cup heavy cream

• three eggs, whisked

• ½ teaspoon turmeric

• five ounces. Monterey Jack cheese, shredded

Directions:

1. Toss the butter withinside the pan and soften it.

2. Add ground red meat, Taco seasoning, and turmeric. Mix up the combination and cook it for 10 mins over the medium warmness or till the ground red meat is cooked.

3. In the bowl, integrate collectively whisked eggs and heavy cream.

4. Transfer the cooked ground red meat combination withinside the pie dish. Pour the egg combination over the ground red meat.

5. Sprinkle the pie with the shredded cheese.

6. Preheat oven to 360F and placed the pie in it.

7. Cook the pie for 10-15 mins or till its miles mild brown.

Nutrition Values: Calories 252, fats 19.2, fiber 0, carbs 1.6, protein 17.5

69. Soup with Meatballs

Preparation time: 15 mins

Cooking time: half-hour

Smart Points: 2

Servings: four

Ingredients:

- 1 teaspoon olive oil
- ½ white onion, diced
- 1 cup ground red meat
- ½ teaspoon ground black pepper
- ½ carrot, grated
- 1 tablespoon almond flour
- four cups of water
- ½ cup heavy cream
- 1/three cup cauliflower, kind of chopped
- 1 teaspoon salt
- 1 tablespoon clean dill, chopped

Directions:

1. Preheat the skillet nicely and pour olive oil internal.

2. Add white onion and cauliflower. Roast the components for five mins. Stir them from time to time.

3. After this, pour water and heavy cream withinside the saucepan. Bring the liquid to boil.

4. Then upload roasted veggies, chopped dill, and salt. Cook it over the low warmness for five mins.

5. Meanwhile, make the meatballs: withinside the blending bowl, blend up collectively ground red meat, ground black pepper, almond flour, and grated carrot. Make the medium length meatballs.

6. Put the meatballs withinside the soup combination and near the lid.

7. Cook the soup for 10 mins over the medium warmness. Then get rid of the soup from the warmth and depart it to relaxation for 10 mins.

8. Ladle it into the serving bowls.

Nutrition Values: Calories 179, fats 14.5, fiber 1.6, carbs 5, protein 7.5

70. Cornbread Casserole

Preparation time: 15 mins

Cooking time: forty mins

Smart Points: 2

Servings: 6

Ingredients:

- 1 ½ cup almond flour
- three eggs, whisked
- three tablespoon heavy cream
- 2 tablespoon butter, melted
- ½ teaspoon baking powder

- three ounces. Cheddar cheese, shredded

- 2 cups ground red meat

- ½ teaspoon ground cumin

- ½ teaspoon salt

- 1 white onion, diced

- 1 tablespoon olive oil

- ¼ teaspoon garlic powder

- 1 teaspoon ground coriander

- five ounces. Parmesan, grated

Directions:

1. Make the cornbread: withinside the blending bowl, blend up collectively almond flour, whisked eggs, heavy cream, butter, and baking powder. Add shredded Cheddar cheese. Stir the combination nicely till homogenous. Leave the combination to relaxation.

2. After this, pour olive oil withinside the skillet. Add ground red meat, ground cumin, salt, diced onion, garlic powder, and ground coriander.

3. Mix up the beef combination nicely and near the lid. Cook it over the medium-low warmness for 10 mins.

4. Meanwhile, preheat the oven to 365F.

5. Spread the baking dish with ½ a part of all cornbread combination.

6. Then upload the layer of ground red meat combination.

7. Add the closing cornbread and unfold it nicely. Sprinkle it over with the grated Parmesan.

8. Transfer the baking dish withinside the oven and cook it for 25 mins.

9. Let the cooked casserole relaxation for 10-15 mins earlier than serving.

Nutrition Values: Calories 379, fats 29.5, fiber 1.2, carbs 6.5, protein 24.5

71. Roasted Tomato Soup

Preparation time: 15 mins

Cooking time: 15 mins

Smart Points: 2

Servings: 2

Ingredients:

- 1 cup tomatoes

- 1/three cup heavy cream

- 1 ½ cup water

- 1 tablespoon Italian seasoning

- 1 teaspoon olive oil

- ½ teaspoon chili flakes

- ½ teaspoon salt

- 1 garlic clove, peeled

Directions:

1. Make the small cuts in tomatoes and vicinity them withinside the tray. Add garlic.

2. Transfer the tray withinside the preheated to 365F oven and cook for 10 mins.

3. Then vicinity baked tomatoes withinside the meals processor. Add water, heavy cream, Italian seasoning, olive oil, chili flakes, and salt.

4. Process the combination till its miles smooth.

5. Transfer the liquid withinside the saucepan and convey it to boil.

6. The soup ought to sit back for five-10 mins earlier than serving.

Nutrition Values: Calories 129, fats 12, fiber 1.1, carbs 5.5, protein 1.5

72. WW Bacon Risotto

Preparation time: 10 mins

Cooking time: 20 mins

Smart Points: four

Servings: four

Ingredients:

- 6 ounces. bacon, chopped
- 2 cups cauliflower, shredded
- ½ cup white mushrooms, chopped
- 1 tablespoon dried cilantro
- ½ teaspoon salt
- ½ teaspoon ground black pepper
- ½ cup heavy cream
- 1/three cup water
- 1 teaspoon olive oil
- 1 teaspoon onion powder

Directions:

1. Place bacon withinside the pan and cook it over the medium warmness for three mins.

2. Then upload mushrooms and cook them for two mins greater.

3. After this, upload cauliflower, dried cilantro, salt, ground black pepper, olive oil, and onion powder. Mix the combination up.

4. Cook it for five mins.

5. Add water and heavy cream.

6. Close the lid and Sauté risotto for 10 mins over the medium-low warmness.

Nutrition Values: Calories 309, fats 24.6, fiber 1.8, carbs 5.5, protein 17.5

73. Easy Lunch Tacos

Preparation Time: 35 mins

Smart Points: 2

Servings: three

Ingredients:

• 1/four cup tomatoes; chopped.

• 2 cups cheddar cheese; grated

• 2 teaspoons sriracha sauce

• 1 small avocado; pitted, peeled and chopped.

• 1 cup favored taco meat; cooked

• Cooking spray

• Salt and black pepper to the taste.

Directions:

1. Spray a few cooking oil on coated baking dish.

2. Spread cheddar cheese at the baking sheet, introduce withinside the oven at four hundred levels F and bake for 15 mins

3. Spread taco meat over cheese and bake for 10 mins greater

4. Meanwhile; in a bowl, blend avocado with tomatoes, sriracha sauce, salt and pepper and stir.

5. Spread this over taco and cheddar layers, depart tacos to quiet down a bit, slice the usage of a pizza slicer and serve for lunch.

Nutrition Values: Calories:399; Fat : 23; Fiber : 0; Carbs : 2; Protein : 37

74. Special Lunch Dish

Preparation Time: 25 mins

Smart Points: 2

Servings: 2

Ingredients:

• 1-pound red meat; ground

• 2 red meat warm puppies; finely chopped.

• 1½ cups cheddar cheese; shredded

• 1½ cups cheese combo

• A drizzle of olive oil

• 1/four teaspoon paprika

• 1/four teaspoon onion powder

• 1/four teaspoon garlic powder

• 1 cup lettuce leaves; chopped.

• 1/four teaspoon antique bay

• 1 tablespoon thousand island dressing

• 2 tablespoons dill pickle; chopped.

• 2 tablespoons yellow onion; chopped.

• half of cup American cheese; shredded

• Some ketchup for serving

• Some mustard for serving

• Salt and black pepper to the taste.

Directions:

1. Heat up a pan with a drizzle of oil over medium warmness; upload 1/2 of the cheese combo, unfold into a circle and pinnacle with 1/2 of the cheddar cheese

2. Also unfold into a circle, cook for five mins, switch to a reducing board and depart apart for a couple of minutes to quiet down.

3. Heat up the pan once more, upload the relaxation of the cheese combo and unfold into a circle

4. Add the relaxation of the cheddar, additionally unfold, cook for five mins and additionally switch to a reducing board.

5. Spread the thousand islands dressing over the two pizza crusts

6. Heat up the equal pan once more over medium warmness; upload red meat; stir and brown for a couple of minutes

7. Add salt, pepper, antique bay seasoning, paprika, onion and garlic powder; stir and cook for a couple of minutes greater

8. Add warm puppies' portions; stir and cook for five mins greater

9. Spread lettuce, pickles, American cheese and onions on the two pizza crusts

10. Divide red meat and warm canine blend, drizzle mustard and ketchup on the give up and serve

Nutrition Values: Calories: 200; Fat : 6; Fiber :2.5; Carbs : 1.9; Protein : 10

75. Delightful Bacon Wrapped Sausages

Preparation Time: forty mins

Smart Points: three

Servings: four

Ingredients:

• eight bacon strips

• eight sausages

• 1 pinch of onion powder

• sixteen pepper jack cheese slices

• A pinch of garlic powder

• half of teaspoon candy paprika

• Salt and black pepper to the taste.

Directions:

1. Heat up your kitchen grill over medium warmness; upload sausages, cook for a couple of minutes on every

aspect, switch to a plate and depart them apart for a couple of minutes to quiet down.

2. Cut a slit withinside the center of every sausage to create pockets, stuff every with 2 cheese slices and season with salt, pepper, paprika, onion and garlic powder.

3. Wrap every crammed sausage in a bacon strip, stable with toothpicks, vicinity on a coated baking sheet, introduce withinside the oven at four hundred levels F and bake for 15 mins

4. Serve warm for lunch!

Nutrition Values: Calories: 500; Fat: 37; Fiber : 12; Carbs : 3.5; Protein :39.5

76. Yummy Green Soup

Preparation Time: 23 mins

Smart Points: three

Servings: 6

Ingredients:

• 1 cauliflower head, florets separated

• 1 white onion, finely chopped.

• 1 bay leaf, crushed.

• 2 garlic cloves, minced

• five oz watercress

• 1-quart veggie inventory

• 1 cup coconut milk

• 7 oz spinach leaves

• 1/four cup ghee

• A handful parsley, for serving

• Salt and black pepper to the taste.

Directions:

1. Heat up a pot with the ghee over medium excessive warmness; upload garlic and onion; stir and brown for four mins

2. Add cauliflower and bay leaf; stir and cook for five mins

3. Add watercress and spinach; stir and cook for three mins

4. Add inventory, salt and pepper; stir and convey to a boil.

5. Add coconut milk; stir, take off warmness and mix the usage of an immersion blender.

6. Divide into bowls and serve proper away.

Nutrition Values: Calories: 230; Fat : 34; Fiber :2.9; Carbs :4.5; Protein : 7

77. Buffalo Wings

Preparation Time: half-hour

Smart Points: 2

Servings: 2

Ingredients:

- 6 fowl wings, reduce in halves

- A pinch of garlic powder

- half of cup warm sauce

- half of teaspoon candy paprika

- 2 tablespoons ghee

- A pinch of cayenne pepper

- Salt and black pepper to the taste.

Directions:

1. In a bowl, blend fowl portions with 1/2 of the new sauce, salt and pepper and toss nicely to coat.

2. Arrange fowl portions on a coated baking dish, introduce in preheated broiler and broil eight mins

3. Flip fowl portions and broil for eight mins greater

4. Heat up a pan with the ghee over medium warmness.

5. Add the relaxation of the new sauce, salt, pepper, cayenne and paprika; stir and cook for a couple of mins

6. Transfer broiled fowl portions to a bowl, upload ghee and warm sauce blend over them and toss to coat nicely.

7. Serve them proper away!

Nutrition Values: Calories: 500; Fat: 44; Fiber : 12; Carbs : 1; Protein :45.5

78. WW Lunch Burgers

Preparation Time: 35 mins

Smart Points: 2

Servings: eight

Ingredients:

- 1-pound red meat; ground

- 1 pound brisket; ground

- 1 tablespoon ghee

- 2 tablespoons olive oil

- 1 yellow onion; chopped.

- 1 tablespoon water

- eight butter slices

- 1 tablespoon garlic; minced

- 1 tablespoon Italian seasoning

- 2 tablespoons mayonnaise

- Salt and black pepper to the taste.

Directions:

1. In a bowl, blend brisket with red meat, salt, pepper, Italian seasoning, garlic and mayo and stir nicely.

2. Shape eight patties and make a pocket in every.

3. Stuff every burger with a butter slice and seal.

4. Heat up a pan with the olive oil over medium warmness; upload onions; stir and cook for two mins

5. Add the water; stir and acquire them withinside the nook of the pan.

6. Place burgers withinside the pan with the onions and cook them over medium-low warmness for 10 mins

7. Flip them, upload the ghee and cook them for 10 mins greater

eight. Divide burgers on buns and serve them with caramelized onions on pinnacle.

Nutrition Values: Calories:175; Fat :7.5; Fiber: 1; Carbs :3.9; Protein: 20

79. Enchilada Bowl

Preparation time: 10 mins

Cooking time: half-hour

Smart Points: four

Servings: 2

Ingredients:

• 1 cup cauliflower, shredded

• 10 ounces. fowl breast, skinless, boneless

• 1 tablespoon Enchilada sauce

• 1 jalapeno pepper, chopped

• 1 bell pepper, chopped

• ½ cup of water

• ½ teaspoon ground black pepper

• ½ white onion, diced

Directions:

1. Pour water withinside the pan and convey it to boil.

2. Meanwhile, chop the fowl breast. Add it withinside the boiled water, preserve boiling it.

3. After 10 mins of cooking, upload chopped jalapeno pepper and bell pepper.

4. Then upload ground black pepper and diced onion.

5. Mix up the components nicely, near the lid and sauté them for five mins.

6. Then upload shredded cauliflower and Enchilada sauce. Mix it up.

7. Sauté the meal for 10 mins over the medium-low warmness.

Nutrition Values: Calories 210, fats four, fiber three.1, carbs 10.5, protein 32.1

80. Stuffed Tomatoes with Tuna

Preparation time: 10 mins

Cooking time: 15 mins

Smart Points: 2

Servings: five

Ingredients:

- five tomatoes

- 10 ounces. tuna, drained

- five tablespoon cream cheese

- ½ teaspoon garlic clove, diced

- ½ teaspoon cayenne pepper

- 1 teaspoon dried dill

- four ounces. Provolone cheese, shredded

Directions:

1. Cut the tomato caps and scoop down the flesh.

2. In the combination bowl, blend up collectively cream cheese, diced garlic, cayenne pepper, and dried dill.

3. Churn the combination and upload shredded cheese with tuna.

4. Mix it up.

5. Fill the tomatoes with tuna combination and cowl with the tomato caps.

6. Wrap each tomato withinside the foil and vicinity withinside the tray.

7. Cook the tomatoes withinside the preheated to the 365F oven for 15 mins.

Nutrition Values: Calories 244, fats 14.5, fiber 1.6, carbs 5.5, protein 22.6

81. Eggplant Panini

Preparation time: 10 mins

Cooking time: 10 mins

Smart Points: three

Servings: four

Ingredients:

- 2 eggplants

- 1 tomato, slices

- 1 cup clean spinach

- ½ teaspoon minced garlic

- five ounces. Parmesan, shredded

- 1 tablespoon cream cheese

- 1 teaspoon butter

Directions:

1. Trim eggplants and reduce them along. You want to get four slices from each eggplant.

2. In the combination bowl, blend up collectively cream cheese and minced garlic.

3. Preheat grill nicely.

4. Place the eggplant slices at the grill and cook them for 2.5 mins from every aspect.

5. Transfer the cooked eggplants at the slicing board.

6. Spread four eggplant slices with cream cheese combination.

7. Add sliced tomato, spinach leaves, and shredded Parmesan. Cover the eggplants with the closing eggplant slices.

8. Transfer the eggplant panini (sandwiches in the panini press (grill and cook for two mins or till the cheese is melted.

9. Spread the cooked panini with butter from every aspect and pin with a toothpick.

Nutrition Values: Calories 205, fats 10, fiber 10, carbs 18.5, protein 14.7

SEAFOOD

82. Ginger-Spiced Halibut

Serves: 2

Time: 20 mins

Ingredients:

- 1 tablespoon soy sauce 1
- ½ tablespoons mirin
- 1 tablespoon sesame oil
- 1 teaspoon salt

- three sliced inexperienced onions

- 2 tablespoons clean minced ginger 2 minced garlic cloves

- 10-oz. halibut

Directions:

1.Preheat the oven to 350 stages Fahrenheit (a hundred and eighty stages Celsius).

2. In a big blending bowl, integrate the soy sauce, mirin, sesame oil, salt, onions, ginger, and garlic.

3. Line a baking pan with aluminum foil and set up the salmon fillets within.

4. Drizzle the ginger sauce over pinnacle.

5. Bake for 15 mins, or till the temperature of the fish reaches a hundred forty five stages.

6. Immediately region it at the table!

Nutrition: calories: 226 Carbs: eight Protein: 28 Fat: 9Fiber: zero

83. Baked Tilapia Spinach

Serves: four

Time: 20-23 mins

Ingredients:

Fish:

• 1-pound clean spinach

• four teaspoons extra-virgin olive oil

• 1 teaspoon garlic powder

• Four (6-ounce) fillets of tilapia Salt to taste

Sauce:

• 2 tablespoons rice wine vinegar

• 2 tablespoons coconut aminos

• 1 teaspoon toasted sesame oil

• 2 teaspoons granulated stevia

• ½ teaspoon chili powder

Directions:

1.Preheat the oven to four hundred stages Fahrenheit (two hundred stages Celsius).

2. Using nonstick spray, grease an 18x12 baking pan.

3. Toss in 2 teaspoons olive oil and 12 teaspoon garlic powder into the pan. four. Toss withinside the spinach to blend.

4. Before serving, season the fish with the final oil and garlic.

5 Add a pinch of salt to finish.

6. Bake for 15-18 mins, or till the fish reaches an inner temperature of 160°F.

7. Meanwhile, whisk collectively the sauce elements.

8. Pour the sauce over the fish after it is carried out cooking and serve!

Nutrition: calories: 235 Carbs: 7 Protein: 33 Fat: 10.5 Fiber: 2.9

84. Fish Tacos

Serves: three

Time: 10-15 mins

Ingredients:

• 1 pound chopped Alaskan cod

• 1 teaspoon salt

• 1 teaspoon paprika

• 1 teaspoon cumin

• 1 teaspoon black pepper One lime's really well worth of juice

• corn tortillas

• 1 cup shredded cabbage

• ½ cup chopped tomatoes

• ⅓ cup chopped clean cilantro

• ⅓ cup chopped onion (optional)

Directions:

1. Spray a pan with nonstick cooking spray and warmth till warm over medium-excessive warmth.

2. In a big blending basin, integrate the fish, spices, and lime juice.

3. Cook for 10-15 mins, stirring often, or till the fish is cooked through.

4. Preheat a 2nd skillet at the stovetop at the same time as the primary one is cooking.

5. Add the tortillas to melt them, then circulate them to a chunk of aluminum foil after black spots appear. Once every tortilla has been loaded, wrap it one by one to make sure that it remains warm.

6. To make the tacos, divide the fish among the tortillas and pinnacle with cabbage, tomatoes, cilantro, and onion, if the usage of uncooked onion. Roll them up and serve.

7. Have fun!

Nutrition: calories: 280 Carbs: 28 Protein: 33 Fat: four Fiber: three

85. Honey-Lemon Salmon

Serves: four

Time: 38 mins

Ingredients:

- 1 teaspoon lemon zest
- ¼ cup lemon juice
- 1 tablespoon vegetable oil
- 2 teaspoons honey
- 1 minced garlic clove Pinch of salt
- Pinch of black pepper
- sixteen-oz. salmon
- 2 cups corn kernels
- 1 yellow bell pepper
- ½ cup chopped purple onion

Directions:

1. Combine the zest, juice, oil, honey, garlic, salt, and black pepper in a big blending bowl.

2. Combine three tablespoons of the aggregate with the 4 salmon fillets in a Ziploc bag.

3. Ensure that the fish is very well lined through energetic shaking.

4. Refrigerate the box for at the least half-hour.

5. In a big blending bowl, integrate the corn, pepper, and onion with the final lemon zest aggregate.

6. Refrigerate after absolutely stirring.

7. Spray a baking sheet with nonstick cooking spray and preheat the broiler.

8. Carefully region the fish withinside the pan.

9. Broil for four mins on one aspect, then turn and broil for every other four mins.

10. Cook salmon till it reaches a temperature of 150 stages Fahrenheit.

11. Before serving, toss with the corn, pepper, and onions!

Nutrition: calories: 275 Carbs: 23 Protein: 27 Fat: 10 Fiber: three

86. Garlic and Lemon Mahimahi

Smart Points: 2

Servings: four

Cooking time: 31 mins

Ingredients:

- 1 tablespoon extra-virgin olive oil

- three cloves of garlic, minced

- four four-oz. mahimahi or dolphinfish fillets

- ½ tsp pepper

- Zest from 1 lemon

Directions:

1. Heat oil in a skillet over medium flame and sauté the garlic till fragrant.

2. Add the mahimahi fillets and season with pepper, and lemon zest.

three. Place internal a 3500F preheated oven and cook for half-hour.

Nutrition Values: Calories: 111.1; Carbs: 1.3g; Protein: 21.3g; Fats: 2.3g; Saturated Fat: .5g; Sodium: 131mg

87. Mediterranean Style Fish

Smart Points: 2

Servings: four

Cooking time: 25 mins

Ingredients:

- 2 tablespoons olive oil

- four 6-ounce fish fillets

- 1 big tomato, chopped

- 1 onion, chopped

- ¼ cup pitted olives, low sodium

- 2 tbsp capers

- 1 tablespoon lemon juice

- Salt and pepper to taste

Directions:

1. Preheat the oven to 3500F.

2. Place olive oil withinside the center of a big aluminum foil.

3. Put the fish withinside the center and pinnacle with tomato, onion, olives, and capers.

4. Season with lemon juice, salt and pepper.

5. Fold the aluminum foil and seal the rims through crimping.

6. Place in the oven and cook for 25 mins.

Nutrition Values: Calories: 210.five; Carbs: 6.4g; Protein: 27.1g; Fats: eight.5g; Saturated Fat: 1.2g; Sodium: 282mg

88. Pan-Grilled Fish Steaks

Smart Points: 2

Servings: four

Cooking time: 10 mins

Ingredients:

• 1 tablespoon olive oil

• 1 clove of garlic, minced

• 2 fillets of halibut

• 1 teaspoon dried basil

• 1 teaspoon black pepper

• 1 tablespoon lemon juice, freshly squeezed

• 1 tablespoon clean parsley, chopped

Directions:

1. Heat oil in a skillet over medium warmth and sauté the garlic till fragrant.

2. Stir withinside the halibut and sear all facets for two mins every.

3. Add the basil, pepper, and lemon juice.

4. Continue cooking till the liquid nearly evaporates. Flip the fillet.

5. Cook for five extra mins.

6. Garnish with parsley earlier than serving.

Nutrition Values: Calories: 407.7; Carbs: 1.1g; Protein: 29.5g; Fats: 31.7g; Saturated Fat: five.4g; Sodium: 164mg

89. Pan-Grilled Tuna Burger

Smart Points: three

Servings: 2

Cooking time: 10 mins

Ingredients:

• 1 tail-stop tuna fillet, without pores and skin and chopped

• 1 tablespoon lemon juice

• ½ tsp pepper

• 1 small onion

• 1 tsp garlic powder

• ¼ tsp celery seeds

• ½ tsp Cajun seasoning

• ¼ teaspoon olive oil

• 2 complete wheat burger buns

- 1 tomato, sliced
- 2 lettuce leaf

Directions:

1. Peel onions and slice in 1/2 of widthwise. Slice 1/2 of the onion into and set apart. Chop the alternative 1/2 of the onion.

2. In a bowl, blend nicely chopped tuna, lemon juice, pepper, chopped onion, garlic powder, celery seeds, and Cajun seasoning. Mix nicely and divide into. Form into patties.

3. Heat pan with oil on medium excessive hearthplace and pan fry patties for three mins in line with aspect.

4. To serve, region Pattie on a bun pinnacle with onion and tomato slices and a lettuce leaf.

Nutrition Values: Calories: 110; Carbs: 6.9g; Protein: 14.3g; Fats: three.5g; Saturated Fat: .8g; Sodium: 77mg

90. Indulgent Seafood Enchiladas

Smart Points: 2

Servings: 6

Cooking time: five mins

Ingredients:

- ½ tablespoon olive oil
- 1 onion, chopped
- ½ pound crab meat
- ¼ pound shrimps, peeled and deveined
- Salt and pepper to taste
- 6 complete wheat tortillas
- ½ cup bitter cream, low fat
- eight-ounce Colby cheese, low fat

Directions:

1. Heat the oil in a skillet over medium warmth and sauté the onion till fragrant.

2. Stir withinside the crab meat and shrimps.

3. Season with pepper to taste.

4. Continue stirring for four mins. Set apart.

5. Assemble the enchiladas through placing the seafood aggregate in tortilla wraps.

6. Add butter cream and cheese on pinnacle.

Nutrition Values: Calories: 360; Carbs: 36.5g; Protein: 30.3g; Fats: 10.31g; Saturated Fat: 5.3g; Sodium: 324mg

91. Mouth-Watering Seafood Curry

Smart Points: three

Servings: 6

Cooking time: 10 mins

Ingredients:

• 1 tablespoon olive oil

• 1 onion, chopped

• 2 cloves of garlic, minced

• 1 teaspoon garam masala

• 1 teaspoon turmeric powder

• 1 teaspoon coriander powder

• 12-ounce cod fillets

• ½ pound shrimps, peeled and deveined

• ½ pound scallops

• 2 cups coconut milk

• 1 purple bell pepper, seeded and sliced

• ¼ tsp pepper

Directions:

1. Heat the oil in a pot over medium excessive flame and sauté the onion and garlic till fragrant, round 2 mins.

2. Add the garam masala, turmeric, and coriander. Toast for 1 minute.

3. Stir withinside the relaxation of the elements.

4. Close the lid and produce to a boil.

5. Allow simmering for six mins.

Nutrition Values: Calories: 393.6; Carbs: 7.8g; Protein: 23.2g; Fats: 22.3g; Saturated Fat: 10.4g; Sodium: 305mg

92. Summertime Crab with Napa Cabbage

Smart Points: 2

Servings: 6

Cooking time: zero mins

Ingredients:

• 2 tablespoons lemon juice

• 1 tablespoon olive oil

• 1 tablespoon maple syrup

• Salt and pepper to taste

• 1-pound crabmeat, shredded

• 1 ½ kilos Napa cabbage, shredded

• five stalks of celery, diced

• 6 radishes, sliced thinly

• 2 tbsp black olives, drained, rinsed and sliced

• three inexperienced onions, sliced thinly

Directions:

1. In a small bowl, integrate the lemon juice, olive oil, and maple syrup. Season with pepper to taste. Set apart.

2. Mix all elements in a bowl.

3. Drizzle with the sauce and toss to coat.

4. Chill earlier than serving.

Nutrition Values: Calories: 268; Carbs: 20.4g; Protein: 37.4g; Fats: 5.3g; Saturated Fat: 1.8g; Sodium: mg

93.Salmon with Dill and Lemon

Smart Points: 2

Servings: 2

Cooking time: 20 mins

Ingredients:

• 1/2-pound salmon fillet, reduce into 2 identical portions

• Pepper to taste

• 2 lemons, juice extracted

• 2 sprigs clean dill, chopped

• Cooking spray

Directions:

1. Preheat oven to 400oF.

2. Lightly grease an oven secure dish with cooking spray.

3. Place salmon on dish pores and skin aspect down.

4. Pour lemon juice, season generously with pepper, and pinnacle with dill.

5. Place in oven and bake for 12 to fifteen mins or till flaky.

6. Let salmon relaxation for five mins.

7. Serve and experience.

Nutrition Values: Calories: 199; Carbs: 4.5g; Protein: 24g; Fats: 9g; Saturated Fat: 1.8g; Sodium: 293mg

94. Grilled Prawn Kebab

Smart Points: three

Servings: three

Cooking time: 6 mins

Ingredients:

• 6 big prawns, peeled and deveined

• 2 tablespoons lemon juice

• Pepper to taste

• 1 teaspoon parsley leaves, chopped

• three pineapple slices

Directions:

1. Marinate the prawns in lemon juice, salt and pepper for half-hour withinside the refrigerator.

2. Preheat the grill to medium.

3. Skewer 2 prawns and a pineapple slice on every bamboo skewer.

4. Grill for three mins on every aspect.

Nutrition Values: Calories: 104; Carbs: 21.6g; Protein: 4.8g; Fats: 0.9g; Saturated Fat: 0g; Sodium: 13mg

95. Cioppino – Seafood Stew

Smart Points: 2

Servings: eight

Cooking time: 50 mins

Ingredients:

• three celery sticks, chopped

• 1 purple bell pepper, chopped

• 2 onions, chopped

• 2 cups fish inventory, low sodium

• ½ cup water

• 2 big tomatoes, chopped

• 1 tablespoon garlic, minced

• 2 teaspoons Italian seasoning

• 1 bay leaf

• Pepper to taste

• 1-pound little neck clams

• 1-lb shrimps, shelled and deveined

• 1-lb cod fillet, reduce into 1-inch pieces

• 2 tablespoons basil, chopped

• 1 tablespoon parsley, chopped

• purple pepper flakes to taste

Directions:

1. Place a heavy bottomed pot on medium excessive hearthplace.

2. Add celery, bell pepper, onions, fish inventory, tomatoes, garlic, Italian seasoning, pepper flakes, pepper, fish inventory, Italian seasoning, water and bay leaf. Mix nicely.

3. Bring to a boil, decrease hearthplace to a simmer, cowl and cook for 10 mins.

4. Stir in shrimps and clams. Cover and cook for every other 7 mins.

5. Add fish and basil. Cook for three mins. Let it relaxation for five mins. Do now no longer blend because the fish fillet will crumble.

6. Serve and experience with a sprinkle of parsley.

Nutrition Values: Calories: 172.5; Carbs: 14.5g; Protein: 23.4g; Fats: 2.3g; Saturated Fat: .4g; Sodium: 351mg

96. Stir-Fried Sesame Shrimp

Smart Points: 2

Servings: three

Cooking time: 15 mins

Ingredients:

• ¾ cup bird broth, low sodium

• 1/eight cup cornstarch

• 1/2 -pound sugar snap peas

• 1 tbsp teriyaki sauce

• three inexperienced onions, sliced

• 1 purple bell pepper, sliced into skinny strips

• 2 tsp sesame oil

• ¼ tsp floor black pepper

• 1 tbsp sesame seeds

• 1 clove garlic, minced

• ¼ tsp cayenne pepper

• ¼ tsp floor ginger

• 1-lb medium shrimp, peeled and deveined

Directions:

1. In a big bowl blend black pepper, sesame seeds, cayenne pepper. Ginger, and shrimp. Mix nicely and permit it marinate for at the least half-hour.

2. When ready, region a nonstick saucepan on medium excessive hearthplace and warmth for three mins.

3. Add oil and warmth for a minute. Swirl to coat pot.

4. Add inexperienced onions and bell pepper. Stir fry for four mins.

5. Add shrimp, peas, and teriyaki sauce. Stir fry for five mins or till shrimps are barely opaque.

6. In a bowl, blend broth and cornstarch. Pour into pot and blend nicely.

7. Continue blending and cooking till sauce has thickened.

8. Serve and experience.

Nutrition Values: Calories: 308.6; Carbs: 15.2g; Protein: 37.1g; Fats: 10.6g; Saturated Fat: 2.3g; Sodium: 216mg

97. White Fish in Dijon Sauce

Serves: four

Time: 17 mins

Ingredients:

• sixteen-oz. sole

• 2 tablespoons Dijon mustard

- three teaspoons lemon juice

- 2 teaspoons reduced-sodium

- Worcestershire sauce

- four tablespoons bread crumbs

- 2 teaspoons Italian seasoning

Directions:

1. Preheat the oven to 450 stages Fahrenheit.

2. If the fish hasn't already been split, reduce it into 4 fillets.

3. Grease an 11x7-inch baking dish with cooking spray.

4. Combine the Dijon mustard, lemon juice, and Worcestershire sauce in a blending bowl.

5. Apply a touch coat of oil to the fillets.

6. Sprinkle with bread crumbs and Italian spice and serve.

7. Bake for 12 mins, or till the fish is flaky and the inner temperature is at the least a hundred forty five stages.

8. Make certain to serve it warm!

Nutrition: calories: 140 Carbs: 6 Protein: 21 Fat: 2 Fiber: 1

98. Fried Salmon Cakes

Serves: 6

Time: 28-half-hour

Ingredients:

- 15-oz. canned salmon

- ½ minced onion

- ½ chopped bell pepper

- 1 crushed egg

- ¼ cup bread crumbs

- 1 teaspoon warm sauce Salt to taste

- Black pepper to taste

- 2 teaspoons dried parsley

- 1 teaspoon garlic powder

- ¼ cup flour

- ¼ cup yellow cornmeal

- ½-inch really well worth of vegetable oil

Directions:

1. In a big blending basin, toss the salmon with the onion and pepper till very well incorporated. Add the bread crumbs and highly spiced sauce after seasoning with salt and pepper to taste.

2. Using a spatula, shape into flat desserts.

3. Combine the flour and cornmeal in a separate basin.

4. In a saucepan, warmth the oil till it's far extraordinarily warm.

5. Dredge each facet of the desserts withinside the flour/cornmeal aggregate, then fry till golden brown on each facets, approximately five mins total. It must take not than three-five mins to finish every aspect.

6. Put the meals at the table!

Nutrition: calories: 157 Carbs: 15 Protein: 15.5 Fat: 4.5 Fiber: 1

99. Shrimp Scampi Recipe

Serves: four

Time: 10-12 mins

Ingredients:

• four teaspoons extra-virgin olive oil

• 1 ¼ kilos peeled uncooked shrimp

• minced garlic cloves

• ½ cup dry white wine

• ½ cup low-sodium bird inventory One lemon's really well worth of juice

• 1 teaspoon dry parsley

• ¼ teaspoon salt

• ¼ teaspoon black pepper

Directions:

1. In a pan, warmth the oil over medium warmth till it shimmers.

2. Cook for every other 2-three mins, or till the shrimp are red and company.

3. Cook for 30 seconds after including the garlic, stirring regularly.

4. Place the shrimp on a serving dish and cowl with a paper towel to maintain warm.

5. In a big blending bowl, upload the wine, inventory, lemon juice, and spices.

6. Bring the aggregate to a boil, then lessen the warmth to a low setting.

7. Cook till the sauce has thickened, approximately five mins.

8. Immediately pour the sauce over the shrimp and serve!

Nutrition: calories: 184 Carbs: 6 Protein: 21 Fat: 6 Fiber: 1

100.Shrimp & Tofu Stir Fry

Serves: four

Time: 20-25 mins

Ingredients:

• 1 tablespoon sesame oil

• 1 sliced onion

• 14- oz. cubed extra-company tofu

• minced garlic cloves

- 2 tablespoons oyster sauce

- 1 tablespoon fish sauce

- 1 teaspoon honey

- ½ cup water

- 1 shredded carrot

- 1-pound precooked shrimp

- Pinch of purple pepper flakes

Directions:

1. In a medium saucepan, warmth the sesame oil till it shimmers.

2. Add the onion, tofu, and garlic while the onion, tofu, and garlic are warm.

3. Cook for a similarly five mins, or till the onion begins off evolved to melt.

4. In a blending dish, integrate the oyster sauce, fish sauce, honey, and water.

5. Cook, stirring a couple of times at some point of the process, for 12 mins.

6. Cook for approximately five mins, or till the carrots are not uncooked.

7. Toss withinside the shrimp and cook till very well carried out.

8.Finish with a sprinkling of purple pepper flakes!

Nutrition: calories: 270 Carbs: thirteen Protein: 34 Fat: 10 Fiber: 1

101. Salmon Avocado Salad

Smart Points: 2

Servings: three

Cooking time: 10 mins

Ingredients: s

- 12-ounce salmon fillet

- Salt and pepper to taste

- ½ avocado, thinly sliced

- ¼ cucumber, thinly sliced

- A sprint of lemon juice

- A pinch of dill weed, chopped

- 2 teaspoons capers

Directions:

1. Preheat the grill to medium.

2. Season the salmon with salt and pepper to taste.

3. Grill the salmon for five mins on every aspect. Set apart and permit to cool.

4. Once cooled, flake the salmon the usage of forks.

5. Place in a bowl and toss collectively with the alternative elements.

6. Season with extra salt and pepper if desired.

Nutrition Values: Calories: 118; Carbs: 2.7g; Protein: 12.2g; Fats: 6.6g; Saturated Fat: three.4g; Sodium: 247mg

102. Shrimp and Avocado Salad

Smart Points: 2

Servings: 6

Cooking time: 6 mins

Ingredients:

• 1-pound shrimp, shelled and deveined

• 2 tomatoes, finely chopped

• 1 bunch cilantro, chopped

• 1 purple onion, chopped finely

• 2 avocados, sliced thinly

• 2 tablespoons lemon juice

Directions:

1. Steam the shrimps for six mins. Set apart and permit to cool.

2. In a bowl, integrate the relaxation of the elements.

3. Toss withinside the shrimps and lightly stir.

4. Allow to kick back withinside the refrigerator earlier than serving

Nutrition Values: Calories: 191; Carbs: 7.7g; Protein: 17.6g; Fats: 10.9g; Saturated Fat: three.6g; Sodium: 185mg

103. Simple Tuna and Cucumber Salad

Smart Points: 2

Servings: five

Cooking time: 6 mins

Ingredients:

• ½ pound tuna fillet

• ¼ tsp pepper

• 1 big cucumber, peeled and sliced

• 1 radish, peeled and sliced

• 1 medium-sized tomato, cubed

• 1 purple onion, cubed

• 2 tablespoons lemon juice

• 1 thumb-length ginger, grated

Directions:

1. Season the tuna with pepper.

2. Heat a skillet over medium flame and sear the tuna fillet for three mins every aspect. Slice the tuna into cubes and set apart.

3. In a blending bowl, integrate the relaxation of the elements and toss withinside the sliced tuna.

4. Season with pepper.

Nutrition Values: Calories: 70; Carbs: 7.1g; Protein: 9.9g; Fats: 0.6g; Saturated Fat: 0.1g; Sodium: 89mg

104. Cheesy and Creamy Tilapia

Serves: four

Prep Time: forty mins

Ingredients

- 1 cup Parmesan cheese, grated
- four tilapia fillets
- ¼ cup mayonnaise
- Salt and black pepper, to taste
- ¼ cup clean lemon juice

Directions

1. Preheat the oven to 350 tiers F and grease 2 baking dishes.

2. Marinate tilapia fillets with mayonnaise, clean lemon juice, salt and black pepper.

3. Put the marinated fillets withinside the baking dishes and pinnacle with cheese.

4. Transfer into the oven and bake for approximately half-hour.

5. Remove from the oven and serve warm.

Nutrition

Calories: 245

Carbs: four.9g

Fats: 12.1g

Proteins: 30.4g

Sodium: 411mg

Sugar: 1.3g

105. Roasted Mahi-Mahi Fish

Serves: three

Prep Time: 50 mins

Ingredients

- ½ cup clean lemon juice
- 1 pound mahi-mahi fillets
- four tablespoons butter
- Salt and black pepper, to taste
- 1 teaspoon dried rosemary, crushed

Directions

1. Preheat the oven to 350 tiers F and grease 2 baking dishes.

2. Season the mahi-mahi fish fillets with salt and black pepper.

3. Put the pro fillets withinside the baking dishes and pinnacle with dried oregano, dried rosemary, and clean lemon juice.

4. Bake for approximately half-hour and cast off from the oven to serve warm.

Nutrition

Calories: 267

Carbs: 1.1g

Fats: 15.7g

Proteins: 28.6g

Sodium: 245mg

Sugar: 0.9g

106. Prawns in Gravy

Serves: 6

Prep Time: 20 mins

Ingredients

- four tablespoons butter
- 2 kilos clean prawns, cubed
- 1 big onion, sliced
- Salt and black pepper, to taste

- 1 cup homemade tomato puree

Directions

1. Put the butter and onions in a big skillet and sauté for approximately three mins.

2. Add prawns, tomato puree, salt and black pepper and cook for approximately 12 mins.

3. Dish out and serve warm.

Nutrition

Calories: 268

Carbs: 6.7g

Fats: 10.3g

Proteins: 35.1g

Sodium: 431mg

Sugar: 2.4g

107. Buffalo Fish

Serves: four

Prep Time: 20 mins

Ingredients

- ½ cup Franks pink warm sauce
- four fish fillets
- 1 teaspoon garlic powder
- Salt and black pepper, to taste

- four tablespoons butter

- three tablespoons butter
- three kilos' salmon fillet, cubed
- three medium onions, chopped
- Salt and black pepper, to taste
- three cups homemade fish broth

Directions

1. Marinate the fish fillets with pink warm sauce, garlic powder, salt and black pepper.

2. Refrigerate the marinade for an hour.

3. Put the butter and marinated fish withinside the sluggish cooker.

4. Set the sluggish cooker on LOW and cook for approximately 6 hours.

5. Dish out and serve warm.

Directions

1. Put all of the substances in a sluggish cooker and blend gently.

2. Set the sluggish cooker on LOW and cook for approximately five hours.

3. Dish out and serve warm.

Nutrition

Calories: 317 a

Carbs: 16.2g

Fats: 22.7g

Proteins: 13.6g

Sodium: 671mg

Sugar: 0.2g

Nutrition

Calories: 272

Carbs: four.4g

Fats: 14.2g

Proteins: 32.1g

Sodium: 275mg

Sugar: 1.9g

108. Salmon Stew

Serves: 9

Prep Time: five hours 10 mins

Ingredients

109. Ketogenic Butter Fish

Serves: 6

Prep Time: forty mins

Ingredients

- 6 inexperienced chilies, chopped
- 2 kilos salmon fillets
- 2 cups butter
- Salt and black pepper, to taste
- 12 garlic cloves, finely chopped

Directions

1. Preheat the oven to 360 tiers F and grease 2 baking dishes.

2. Season the salmon fillets with garlic, salt and black pepper.

3. Top with butter and switch into the oven.

4. Bake for approximately half-hour and cast off from the oven to serve warm.

Nutrition

Calories: 565

Carbs: 1.8g

Fats: 53.1g

Proteins: 22.8g

Sodium: 378mg

Sugar: 0.2g

110. Sweet and Sour Fish

Serves: 6

Prep Time: 25 mins

Ingredients

- ¼ cup butter
- 2 kilos fish chunks
- 2 tablespoons vinegar
- Salt and black pepper, to taste
- four drops liquid stevia

Directions

1. Put the butter and fish in a skillet and sauté for approximately four mins.

2. Pour withinside the stevia, vinegar, salt and black pepper.

3. Cook for approximately 10 mins on medium low warmth and dish out to serve warm.

Nutrition

Calories: 190

Carbs: 2.8g

Fats: 9g

Proteins: 27.1g

Sodium: 595mg

Sugar: 2.7g

111. Creamy Shrimp and Bacon

Serves: three

Prep Time: 20 mins

Ingredients

- 1 tablespoon olive oil
- 1-pound uncooked shrimp
- 2 bacon slices
- Salt and black pepper, to taste
- ¼ cup coconut cream

Directions

1. Season the shrimp with salt and black pepper.

2. Put the olive oil and pro shrimp in a non-stick pan.

3. Sauté for approximately five mins and upload bacon and coconut cream.

4. Cook for approximately eight mins and dish out to serve.

Nutrition

Calories: 334

Carbs: three.6g

Fats: 17.3g

Proteins: 39.6g

Sodium: 665mg

Sugar: 0.7g

112. Lemon Garlic Shrimp

Serves: three

Prep Time: 25 mins

Ingredients

- three tablespoons butter
- 1-pound big uncooked shrimp
- 2 lemons, sliced
- 1 teaspoon paprika
- four garlic cloves

Directions

1. Heat the butter in a skillet and upload garlic.

2. Sauté for approximately 1 minute and upload shrimp, paprika, and lemon slices.

3. Cook for approximately 10 mins on medium low warmth and dish out to serve warm.

Nutrition

Calories: 271

Carbs: 6.5g

Fats: 13.4g

Proteins: 32.5g

Sodium: 422mg

Sugar: 1.1g

Sides and Snacks

113.Keto Sausage Balls

Serves: 6

Prep Time: 30 mins

Ingredients

- 1 cup almond flour, blanched
- 1 pound bulk Italian sausage
- 1¼ cups sharp cheddar cheese, shredded
- 2 teaspoons baking powder
- 1 huge egg

Directions

1. Preheat the oven to 360 levels F and grease a baking sheet.

2. Mix collectively all of the components in a huge bowl till properly incorporated.

3. Make same sized balls from this combination and set up at the baking sheet.

4. Transfer withinside the oven and bake for approximately 20 mins till golden brown.

Nutrition

Calories: 477

Carbs: 6.1g

Fats: 39g

Proteins: 25.6g

Sodium: 732mg

Sugar: 0.2g

114.Keto Pistachio Truffles

Serves: five

Prep Time: 10 mins

Ingredients

- ¼ teaspoon natural vanilla extract
- ¼ cup pistachios, chopped
- 1 cup mascarpone cheese, softened
- three tablespoons erythritol s

Directions

1. Mix collectively mascarpone cheese, vanilla, and erythritol in a small bowl.

2. Mix very well till clean and shape small balls out of this combination.

3. Roll the desserts in a plate complete of chopped pistachios

and refrigerate for half-hour earlier than serving.

Nutrition

Calories: 103

Carbs: 11.3g

Fats: 7.8g

Proteins: 6.2g

Sodium: 58mg

Sugar: 9.4g

115. Keto Gin Cocktail

Serves: 1

Prep Time: 10 mins

Ingredients

- four blueberries
- 2 oz dry gin
- 1 teaspoon erythritol, powdered
- 1 can membership soda
- ½ ounce clean lime juice

Directions

1. Put the blueberries and mint right into a cocktail shaker.

2. Shake properly and upload the gin, lime juice, erythritol and ice.

3. Shake once more and pressure right into a cocktail glass.

4. Top with membership soda and serve chilled.

Nutrition

Calories: 161

Carbs: 7.3g

Fats: 0.1g

Proteins: 0.2g

Sodium: 76mg

Sugar: 1.7g

116. Parmesan and Garlic Keto Crackers

Serves: four

Prep Time: forty mins

Ingredients

- 1 cup Parmesan cheese, finely grated
- 1 cup almond flour, blanched

- ½ teaspoon garlic powder
- 1 huge egg, whisked
- 1 tablespoon butter, melted

Directions

1. Preheat the oven to 350 levels F and grease 2 huge baking sheets.

2. Mix collectively the parmesan cheese, almond flour, chives and garlic powder in a huge bowl till properly incorporated.

3. Whisk collectively the eggs and butter in a separate bowl.

4. Mix collectively the dry and moist components till a dough is formed.

5. Divide the dough into halves and press till ¼ inch thick.

6. Cut every sheet of dough with a pastry cutter into 25 crackers of same size.

7. Arrange the crackers at the baking sheets and switch into the oven.

8. Bake for approximately 15 mins and permit them to live withinside the off oven.

9. Remove from the oven and serve.

Nutrition

Calories: 304

Carbs: 7.4g

Fats: 23.5g

Proteins:14.8g

Sodium: 311mg

Sugar: 0.2g

117.Low Carb Dried Cranberries

Serves: four

Prep Time: four hours 15 mins

Ingredients

- 1 cup granular erythritol
- ½ teaspoon natural orange extract
- 2 (12 ounce) luggage clean cranberries, rinsed and dried
- four tablespoons avocado oil

Directions

1. Preheat the oven to 2 hundred levels F and grease a huge baking sheet.

2. Slice the dried cranberries in 1/2 of and placed right into a bowl together with the closing components.

3. Toss to coat properly and set up the berries withinside the baking sheet.

4. Bake for approximately four hours and dish out to serve.

Nutrition

Calories: 111

Carbs: 14.3g

Fats: 1.8g

Proteins: 0.2g

Sodium: 1mg

Sugar: 6.2g

118. Broccoli Cheese Soup

Serves: 6

Prep Time: five hours 10 mins

Ingredients

- 1 cup heavy whipping cream
- 2 cups fowl broth
- 2 cups broccoli

- Salt, to taste
- 2 cups cheddar cheese

Directions

1) Place the cheddar cheese, broccoli, fowl broth, heavy whipping cream and salt in a crock pot.

2) Set the crock pot on LOW and cook for approximately five hours.

3) Ladle out in a bowl and serve hot.

Nutrition Calories: 244 Carbs: 5.3g Fats: 20.4g Proteins: 12.3g Sodium: 506mg Sugar: 1g

119.Mediterranean Spinach with Cheese

Serves: 6

Prep Time: 25 mins

Ingredients

- 2 kilos spinach, chopped
- ½ cup black olives, halved and pitted
- Salt and black pepper, to taste

- four tablespoons butter

- 1½ cups feta cheese, grated

- four teaspoons clean lemon zest, grated

Directions

1) Preheat the Air fryer to four hundred levels F and grease an Air fryer basket.

2) Cook spinach for approximately four mins in a pan of boiling water. Drain properly.

3) Mix collectively butter, spinach, salt, and black pepper in a bowl.

4) Transfer the spinach combination into an air fryer basket.

5) Cook for approximately 15 mins, tossing as soon as withinside the center way.

6) Dish right into a bowl and stir withinside the olives, cheese, and lemon zest to serve.

Nutrition Calories: 215 Carbs: 8g Fats: 17.5g Proteins: 9.9g Sodium: 690mg Sugar: 2.3g

120.Scallion Cake

Serves: four

Prep Time: 30 mins

Ingredients

- ¼ cup flax seeds meal

- ½ cup Parmesan cheese, grated finely

- ½ teaspoon baking powder

- ½ cup low-fats cottage cheese

- 1/three cup scallion, sliced thinly

- ½ cup almond meal

- ¼ cup dietary yeast flakes

- 6 natural eggs, beaten

- ½ cup uncooked hemp seeds

- Salt, to taste

Directions

1) Preheat the oven to 390 levels F and grease four ramekins with oil.

2) Mix collectively salt, baking powder, almond meal, hemp seeds and flax seeds meal in a huge bowl.

3) Mix cottage cheese and eggs in any other bowl and switch this combination into almond meal combination.

4) Mix till properly blended and lightly upload scallions.

5) Transfer the combination flippantly into ramekins and bake for approximately 20 mins.

6) Remove from the oven and serve warm.

Nutrition Calories: 306 Carbs: 10.7g Fats: 19.7g Proteins: 23.5g Sodium: 398mg Sugar: 1.3g

121. Avocado Chips

Serves: 2

Prep Time: 20 mins

Ingredients

- 2 uncooked avocados, peeled and sliced in chips shape

- 2 tablespoons butter

- Salt and freshly floor pepper, to taste

Directions

1) Preheat the oven to 365 levels F and grease a baking dish.

2) Top with butter and avocado slices and switch into the oven.

3) Bake for approximately 10 mins and season with salt and black pepper to serve.

Nutrition Calories: 391 Carbs: 15g Fats: 38.2g Proteins: 4.5g Sodium: 96mg Sugar: 0.5g

122. Cheesy Cauliflower

Serves: 6

Prep Time: 30 mins

Ingredients

- 2 tablespoons mustard

- ½ cup butter, reduce into small portions

- 2 cauliflower heads, chopped

- 1 cup Parmesan cheese, grated

- 2 teaspoons avocado mayonnaise

Directions

1) Preheat the oven to four hundred levels F and grease a baking dish.

2) Mix collectively mustard and avocado mayonnaise in a bowl.

3) Coat the cauliflower with the mustard combination and switch right into a baking dish.

4) Top with Parmesan cheese and butter and bake for approximately 25 mins.

5) Pull from the oven and serve hot.

Nutrition Calories: 201 Carbs: 6.2g Fats: 18.9g Proteins: 5.3g Sodium: 192mg Sugar: 2.4g

123.Parmesan Roasted Bamboo Sprouts

Serves: 6

Prep Time: 25 mins

Ingredients

- 2 cups Parmesan cheese, grated
- 2 kilos bamboo sprouts
- four tablespoons butter
- ½ teaspoon paprika
- Salt and black pepper, to taste

Directions

1) Preheat the oven to 365 levels F and grease a baking dish.

2) Marinate the bamboo sprouts with paprika, butter, salt, and black pepper, and preserve aside.

3) Transfer the pro bamboo sprouts withinside the baking dish and region withinside the oven.

4) Bake for approximately 15 mins and dish to serve.

Nutrition Calories: 162 Carbs: 5.6g Fats: 11.7g Proteins: 7.5g Sodium: 248mg Sugar: 1.4g

124.Mexican Cheesy Veggies

Serves: four

Prep Time: forty mins

Ingredients

- 1 onion, thinly sliced
- 1 tomato, thinly sliced

- 1 zucchini, sliced

- 1 teaspoon combined dried herbs

- Salt and black pepper, to taste

- 1 teaspoon olive oil

- 1 cup Mexican cheese, grated

Directions

1) Preheat the oven to 370 levels F and grease a baking dish.

2) Layer the greens withinside the baking dish and drizzle with olive oil.

3) Top flippantly with cheese and sprinkle with herbs, salt, and black pepper.

4) Bake for approximately half-hour and dish to serve hot.

Nutrition Calories: 305 Carbs: 7.3g Fats: 22.3g Proteins: 15.2g Sodium: 370mg Sugar: 5.2g

125. Green Beans with Mushrooms and Bacons

Serves: four

Prep Time: 25 mins

Ingredients

- four tablespoons onion, minced

- four tablespoons butter

- 1 teaspoon garlic, minced

- four cooked bacon slices, crumbled

- 2 cups frozen inexperienced beans

- 2 (eight-ounce) package deal white mushrooms, sliced

- ¼ teaspoon salt

Directions

1) Put the butter, onions and garlic withinside the Instant Pot and select "Sauté."

2) Sauté for approximately 2 mins and upload in bacon and salt.

3) Close the lid and cook at "High" and "Manual" strain for approximately 10 mins.

4) Select "Cancel" and punctiliously do a herbal release.

5) Remove the lid and stir in beans and mushrooms.

6) Lock the lid once more and cook at "High" and "Manual" strain for approximately 7 mins.

7) Transfer to a bowl and serve hot.

Nutrition Calories: 220 Carbs: 11.6g Fats: 17g Proteins: 10g Sodium: 488mg Sugar: 5.2g

126.Cauliflower Mash

Serves: four

Prep Time: 20 mins

Ingredients

- 1 tablespoon complete-fats coconut milk
- three garlic cloves, minced
- 1 teaspoon inexperienced chilies, chopped
- three tablespoons butter
- ½ cup feta cheese
- 1 head cauliflower stems, absolutely removed
- Salt and black pepper, to taste

Directions

1) Preheat the oven to 360 levels F and grease a baking dish.

2) Place cauliflower portions withinside the baking dish and switch into the oven.

3) Bake for approximately 10 mins and dish out the cauliflower portions.

4) Mix with the closing components and mix with an immersion hand blender to obtain the favored texture.

Nutrition Calories: 154 Carbs: 4.9g Fats: 12.5g Proteins: four.3g Sodium: 292mg Sugar: 2.5g

127. Bacon Wrapped Asparagus

Serves: three

Prep Time: 30 mins

Ingredients

- 6 small asparagus spears
- three bacon slices
- 2 tablespoons butter
- ¼ cup heavy whipping cream

- Salt and black pepper, to taste

Directions

1) Preheat the oven to 370 levels F and grease the baking dish with butter.

2) Sprinkle the asparagus spears with salt and black pepper.

3) Add heavy whipping cream to the asparagus and wrap with bacon slices.

4) Place the wrapped asparagus withinside the baking dish and switch into the oven.

5) Bake for approximately 20 mins and dish out to serve hot.

Nutrition Calories: 176 Carbs: 1.2g Fats: 12.4g Proteins: 0.8g Sodium: 321mg Sugar: 0.5g

128.Cheesy Brussels Sprout

Serves: five

Prep Time: 35 mins

Ingredients

- 1 pound Brussels sprouts
- three tablespoons olive oil
- ½ cup cream
- Salt and black pepper, to taste
- 2 tablespoons butter
- ½ cup parmesan cheese, grated

Directions

1) Preheat the oven to 360 levels F and grease a baking dish.

2) Mix collectively Brussels sprouts, olive oil, parmesan cheese, salt, and black pepper in a bowl.

3) Transfer the Brussels sprouts withinside the baking dish and drizzle with butter.

4) Transfer it into the oven and bake for approximately 25 mins.

5) Dish to serve hot.

Nutrition Calories: 165. Carbs: 7.65g Fats:15.9g Proteins: 5g Sodium: 124mg Sugar: 2g

129. Tomato Soup

Serves: four

Prep Time: 30 mins

Ingredients

- 2 cups low-sodium vegetable broth
- ¼ cup clean basil, chopped
- 1 garlic clove, minced
- 1 teaspoon dried parsley, crushed
- Freshly floor black pepper, to taste
- 1 teaspoon dried basil, crushed
- 2 tablespoons Erythritol
- ½ tablespoon balsamic vinegar
- ½ tablespoon olive oil
- 1-pound clean tomatoes, chopped
- 1 cup cheddar cheese

Directions

1) Put the oil in a pot and upload tomatoes, garlic, herbs, black pepper, and broth.

2) Cover the lid and cook for approximately 18-20 mins on medium-low heat.

3) Stir in sugar and vinegar and region the combination in an immersion blender.

4) Blend till clean and ladle right into a bowl.

5) Garnish with basil and serve immediately.

Nutrition Calories: 194 Carbs: 4.5g Fats: 15.4g Proteins: 9.2g Sodium: 257mg Sugar: 4.5g

130.Spinach Quiche

Serves: 6

Prep Time: 50 mins

Ingredients

- 1 tablespoon butter, melted
- Salt and black pepper, to taste
- 1 (10-ounce) package deal frozen spinach, thawed
- five natural eggs, beaten
- three cups Monterey Jack cheese, shredded

Directions

1) Preheat the oven to 360 levels F and grease a 9-inch pie dish lightly.

2) Put butter and spinach in a huge skillet on medium-low heat.

3) Cook for approximately three mins and set aside.

4) Mix collectively Monterey Jack cheese, spinach, eggs, salt, and black pepper in a bowl.

5) Put the combination into organized pie dish and switch into the oven.

6) Bake for approximately half-hour and eliminate from the oven.

7) Cut into same sized wedges and serve hot.

Nutrition Calories: 349 Carbs: 4.2g Fats: 27.8g Proteins: 23g Sodium: 532mg Sugar: 1.3g

131.Cheese Casserole

Serves: 6

Prep Time: forty mins

Ingredients

- 10-ounce parmesan, shredded

- sixteen-ounce marinara sauce

- 2 tablespoons olive oil

- 2 kilos sausage scramble

- sixteen-ounce mozzarella cheese, shredded

Directions

1) Preheat the oven to 395 levels F and grease olive oil at the baking dish.

2) Arrange 1/2 of the sausage scramble withinside the baking dish and layer with 1/2 of the marinara sauce.

3) Top with 1/2 of the mozzarella and Parmesan cheese.

4) Layer with the closing 1/2 of the sausage scramble and unfold the closing 1/2 of Parmesan and mozzarella cheese.

5) Top with relaxation of the marinara sauce and bake withinside the oven for approximately 25 mins.

6) Dish onto a casserole and serve hot.

Nutrition Calories: 521 Carbs: 6g Fats: 38.8g Proteins: 35.4g Sodium: 201mg Sugar: 4.9g

132. Mixed Nuts

Serves: 15

Prep Time: 25 mins

Ingredients

- 1 cup uncooked peanuts
- Salt, to taste
- 1 cup uncooked almonds
- 1 tablespoon butter, melted
- ½ cup uncooked cashew nuts

Directions

1) Preheat the oven at 330 levels F and grease a baking dish.

2) Put the peanuts, almonds and cashew nuts in a baking dish and switch into the oven.

3) Bake for approximately 12 mins, tossing two times in between.

4) Dish out the nuts from the oven right into a bowl and upload salt and melted butter.

5) Toss to coat properly and go back the nuts combination to the oven.

6) Bake for approximately five extra mins and dish out to serve.

Nutrition Calories: 189 Carbs: 6.6g Fats: 15.5g Proteins: 6.8g Sodium: 19mg Sugar: 1.3g

133. Broccoli Pops

Serves: 6

Prep Time: 20 mins

Ingredients

- 1/4 cup Parmesan cheese, grated
- 2 cups cheddar cheese, grated
- Salt and black pepper, to taste
- three eggs, beaten
- three cups broccoli florets
- 1 tablespoon olive oil

Directions

1) Preheat the oven to 360 levels F and grease a baking dish with olive oil.

2) Pulse the broccoli in a meals processor till finely crumbed.

3) Add broccoli and stir in relaxation of the components in a huge bowl.

4) Make small same-sized balls from the combination.

5) Put the balls in a baking sheet and refrigerate for as a minimum half-hour.

6) Place balls withinside the baking dish and switch the dish into the oven.

7) Bake for approximately thirteen mins and dish out to serve.

Nutrition Calories: 162 Carbs: 1.9g Fats: 12.4g Proteins: 11.2g Sodium: 263mg Sugar: 0.5g

134. Asparagus Bites

Serves: 6

Prep Time: 20 mins

Ingredients

- 1 cup desiccated coconut
- 2 cups asparagus
- 1 cup feta cheese

Directions

1) Preheat the oven to four hundred levels F and grease a baking dish with cooking spray.

2) Place the desiccated coconut in a shallow dish and coat asparagus flippantly with coconut.

3) Arrange the covered asparagus withinside the baking dish and pinnacle with cheese.

4) Transfer into the oven and bake for approximately 10 mins to serve.

Nutrition Calories: 145 Carbs: 5g Fats: 10.3g Proteins: 7g Sodium: 421mg Sugar: 4.5 g

135. Creamy Basil Baked Sausage

Serves: 12

Prep Time: forty-five mins

Ingredients

- eight ounces cream cheese
- three kilos Italian fowl sausages
- ¼ cup basil pesto
- eight ounces mozzarella cheese
- ¼ cup heavy cream

Directions

1. Preheat the oven to four hundred levels F and grease a huge casserole dish.

2. Put the sausages withinside the casserole dish and switch into the oven.

3. Bake for approximately half-hour and dish out.

4. Mix collectively the pesto, cream cheese and heavy cream in a bowl.

5. Top the sausage with the pesto combination, accompanied with the aid of using mozzarella cheese.

6. Bake for 10 extra mins and eliminate from the oven to serve.

Nutrition

Calories: 342

Carbs: 7.9g

Fats: 23.3g

Proteins: 21.6g

Sodium: 624mg

Sugar: 0.5g

136. Low Carb Tortilla Chips

Serves: four

Prep Time: 25 mins

Ingredients

- 2 tablespoons olive oil
- three tablespoons lime juice
- 1 tablespoon taco seasoning
- 6 tortillas, low carb

Directions

1. Preheat the oven to 350 levels F and grease a cookie sheet.

2. Cut every tortilla into small wedges and set up on a cookie sheet.

3. Mix collectively the olive oil and lime juice and spray every tortilla wedge.

4. Sprinkle with the taco seasoning and switch into the oven.

5. Bake for approximately eight mins and rotate the pan.

6. Bake for any other eight mins and dish out to serve.

Nutrition

Calories: 147

Carbs: 17.8g

Fats: 8g

Proteins: 2.1g

Sodium: 174mg

Sugar: 0.7g

137. Salmon Mousse Cucumber Rolls

Serves: 2

Prep Time: 30 mins

Ingredients

- 2 cucumbers, thinly sliced lengthwise
- four ounces smoked salmon
- 1 tablespoon dill, clean
- eight ounces cream cheese
- ½ lemon

Directions

1. Mix collectively the salmon, dill, cream cheese, and lemon in a bowl and mash very well.

2. Apply this combination to the cucumber slices and roll lightly to serve.

Nutrition

Calories: 515

Carbs: 15.2g

Fats: 42.4g

Proteins: 21.4g

Sodium: 1479mg

Sugar: 4.6g

138. Italian keto plate

Serves: three

Prep Time: 10 mins

Ingredients

- 7 oz. prosciutto, sliced
- 1/three cup olive oil
- Salt and black pepper, to taste
- 7 oz. clean mozzarella cheese
- 10 inexperienced olives

Directions

1. Place the prosciutto, mozzarella cheese, and olives in a serving plate.

2. Drizzle with olive oil and season with salt and black pepper to serve.

Nutrition

Calories: 505

Carbs:4.5 g

Fats: 39.2g

Proteins: 32.5g

Sodium: 1572mg

Sugar: 0g

139. Keto Onion Rings

Serves: four

Prep Time: 20 mins

Ingredients

- 2 huge onions, reduce into ¼ inch slices
- 2 teaspoons baking powder
- Salt, to taste
- 2 cups cream cheese
- 2 eggs

Directions

1) Preheat the oven to 375 levels F and separate the onion slices into jewelry.

2) Mix collectively salt and baking powder in a bowl.

3) Whisk collectively cream cheese and eggs in any other dish.

4) Dredge the onion jewelry into baking powder combination and dip into cream cheese combination.

5) Place the onion jewelry withinside the oven and bake for approximately 10 mins.

6) Dish out to serve hot.

Nutrition Calories: 266 Carbs: 9.9g Fats: 22.5g Proteins: 8g Sodium: 285mg Sugar: 5.5g

140. Mexican Inspired Beef Soup

Serves: 12

Prep Time: 20 mins

Ingredients

- 1-pound grass-fed lean floor red meat

- 2 cups self-made red meat broth

- 1 tablespoon chili powder

- ¼ cup cheddar cheese, shredded

- 10-ounce canned sugar-unfastened diced tomatoes with inexperienced chiles

- 2 garlic cloves, minced

- four-ounce cream cheese

- Salt and black pepper, to taste

- ½ teaspoon olive oil

- ¼ cup heavy cream

- 1 teaspoon floor cumin

Directions

1) Place the oil and red meat withinside the strain cooker and sauté for approximately eight mins.

2) Stir withinside the closing components, besides cheddar cheese, and cowl the lid.

3) Cook at excessive strain for approximately 10 mins and do the herbal strain release.

4) Top with cheddar cheese and serve hot.

Nutrition Calories: 405 Carbs: 6.7g Fats: 26.7g Proteins: 31.1g Sodium: 815mg Sugar: 4.5g

141. Zucchini Cream Cheese Fries

Serves: four

Prep Time: 20 mins

Ingredients

- 1 cup cream cheese

- 1 pound zucchini, sliced into 2 ½-inch sticks

- 2 tablespoons olive oil

- Salt, to taste

Directions

1) Preheat the oven to 380 levels F and grease a baking dish with olive oil.

2) Season the zucchini with salt and coat with cream cheese.

3) Place zucchini withinside the baking dish and switch into the oven.

4) Bake for approximately 10 mins and dish out to serve.

Nutrition Calories: 374 Carbs: 7.1g Fats: 36.6g Proteins: 7.7g Sodium: 294mg Sugar: 2.8g